Dogs of the Railways

"Dogs in Our World" Series

*Police Dogs of Trinidad and Tobago:
A 70-Year History* (Debbie Jacob, 2024)

*We Saved Each Other: How Rescue Dogs Help Us
Through Hardship* (Christopher Dale, 2024)

*Dogs of the Railways: Canine Guardians, Companions
and Mascots Since the 19th Century* (Jill Lenk Schilp, 2023)

*The Force Free Dilemma: Truth and Myths in Modern
Dog Training* (Fallon Wilson, 2023)

Horror Dogs: Man's Best Friend as Movie Monster
(Brian Patrick Duggan, 2023)

*I Know Your Dog Is a Good Dog: A Trainer's Insights on Reactive,
Aggressive or Anxious Behavior* (Linda Scroggins, 2023)

*The Most Painful Choice: A Dog Owner's Story
of Behavioral Euthanasia* (Beth Miller, 2023)

Your Service Dog and You: A Practical Guide (Nicola Ferguson, 2023)

*Dog of the Decade: Breed Trends and What They Mean
in America* (Deborah Thompson, 2022)

*Laboratory Dogs Rescued: From Test Subjects
to Beloved Companions* (Ellie Hansen, 2022)

*Beware of Dog: How Media Portrays
the Aggressive Canine* (Melissa Crawley, 2021)

*I'm Not Single, I Have a Dog: Dating Tales
from the Bark Side* (Susan Hartzler, 2021)

*Dogs in Health Care: Pioneering Animal-Human
Partnerships* (Jill Lenk Schilp, 2019)

*General Custer, Libbie Custer and Their Dogs:
A Passion for Hounds, from the Civil War to Little Bighorn*
(Brian Patrick Duggan, 2019)

*Dog's Best Friend: Will Judy, Founder of National Dog Week
and Dog World Publisher* (Lisa Begin-Kruysman, 2014)

*Man Writes Dog: Canine Themes in Literature,
Law and Folklore* (William Farina, 2014)

*Saluki: The Desert Hound and the English Travelers
Who Brought It to the West* (Brian Patrick Duggan, 2009)

Dogs of the Railways

*Canine Guardians,
Companions and Mascots
Since the 19th Century*

JILL LENK SCHILP

DOGS IN OUR WORLD
Series Editor Brian Patrick Duggan

McFarland & Company, Inc., Publishers
Jefferson, North Carolina

LIBRARY OF CONGRESS CATALOGUING-IN-PUBLICATION DATA

Names: Schilp, Jill Lenk, 1947– author.
Title: Dogs of the railways : canine guardians, companions and mascots since the 19th century / Jill Lenk Schilp.
Description: Jefferson, North Carolina : McFarland & Company, Inc., Publishers, 2024 | Series: Dogs in our world | Includes bibliographical references and index.
Identifiers: LCCN 2023043394 | ISBN 9781476682587 (paperback : acid free paper) ♾
ISBN 9781476651262 (ebook)
Subjects: LCSH: Working dogs—United States—History. | Travel with dogs—United States—History. | Railroads—United States—History. | Railroad travel—United States—History. | BISAC: PETS / Dogs / General | TRANSPORTATION / Railroads / General
Classification: LCC SF428.2 .S35 2023 | DDC 636.730973—dc23/eng/20231117
LC record available at https://lccn.loc.gov/2023043394

BRITISH LIBRARY CATALOGUING DATA ARE AVAILABLE

ISBN (print) 978-1-4766-8258-7
ISBN (ebook) 978-1-4766-5126-2

© 2024 Jill Lenk Schilp. All rights reserved

No part of this book may be reproduced or transmitted in any form or by any means, electronic or mechanical, including photocopying or recording, or by any information storage and retrieval system, without permission in writing from the publisher.

Front cover image: © dezy/Shutterstock

Printed in the United States of America

McFarland & Company, Inc., Publishers
 Box 611, Jefferson, North Carolina 28640
  www.mcfarlandpub.com

To George
The adventure continues.

Raildog:
*A dog who finds a home, family,
and fame on the railroad.*

Table of Contents

Acknowledgments	ix
Preface	1
Introduction	5
1. Owney: Guardian of the Railway Mail Service, 1888–1897	9
2. The Railroad Jacks: Hoboes, Travelers, and Philanthropists, Mid–1880s–1931	22
3. Roxey: The Long Island Railroad Commuter, 1904–1914	33
4. Sheba's Bob: Dog Detective of the Long Island Railroad, 1906–1916	45
5. Annie: The Colorado Southern Railway Ambassador of Kindness, 1934–1948	53
6. Shep: Faithfulness on the Great Northern Railroad, 1931–1942	60
7. Fala: A Raildog Rides the Funeral Train, 1945	68
8. Brownie: The Victorville, California, Railroad Station Mascot, 1943–1945	83
9. Railroad K9 Patrols: Guardians of the Railways, 2022	88
10. Companion Pets Hop on Board, 2015 and Beyond	103
11. International Raildogs, 1953–2016	110
12. Raildogs: Finding the Way Home	119
Appendix: Monuments and Memorials to Raildogs	127
Chapter Notes	129
Bibliography	137
Index	149

Acknowledgments

For over 50 years, the home I share with my spouse has been filled with dogs and trains. I married a railroad man—to be precise, a model railroader. He got a dog lady. It was a perfect match.

The inspiration for this book belongs to my husband George, who introduced me to the world of trains—big trains, miniature trains, and trains that ran through the countless remote areas where we drove just to sit in the car or truck and watch trains. I have traveled dusty roads, outlying regions and busy urban complexes to view trains and listen to my spouse cite the history and mechanics of great steam engines, locomotives, and all things railroad. Through it all, there was always a dog by our side. Our marriage and home has grown rich with dogs, miniature trains of all gauges and sizes, and the necessary equipment, activity, and reading material to support both of our avid pursuits.

I am grateful to the dogs who shared my life for over five decades. Dolly, Chloe, Pinecone, Nuggett, Max, and Junior. My canine family showed me their stories and my own. I also owe a debt of gratitude to many rescue dogs that have passed through my life, abandoned strays who showed resilience in their search for a home. They showed me the redemptive power of second acts. All these dogs taught me that home is wherever you find your family and helped me understand and appreciate the lessons of the raildogs. I identify with the raildogs' search for a home, belonging, and resilience in facing challenges.

I wrote most of this book during the Covid pandemic. I'm grateful for all who were patient with me as I traversed the ups and downs and challenges of writing during the Covid lockdowns. I am thankful to friends who believed in me and encouraged and prodded me to keep going even in difficult times. I thank my writing group in Plano, Texas, who listened to me read some chapters aloud on Zoom and provided encouragement and the fellowship of storytellers. Thanks also to Brian Duggan and McFarland for allowing me the opportunity to tell the dogs

Acknowledgments

of the railways' stories and for their patience. I'm grateful to the Southwest Live Steamer organization, who inspired my interest by introducing me to the magic of actually riding on a model steam railroad and riding on a model steam train. I thank the Fort Collins History Connection for use of the photo of Raildog Annie and to Cynthia Orticio for her outstanding assistance in preparing the manuscript.

Finally, I am grateful to have traveled with these remarkable raildogs as they, each in their way, found a home on the rails.

Jill Lenk Schilp
Richardson, Texas

Preface

I spent my childhood reading books about lost dogs on determined journeys to find their way home. I wondered how dogs could be such faithful navigators in search of a former guardian or home. Even as a young girl, I understood and identified with a dog's earnest quest for home and a longing for connection

After college, I married a railroad man. To be precise, he was a model railroader who was as passionate about diminutive locomotives and tiny rolling train stock as I was about big pooches, dog travels, and stories of canine adventures.

Every home we shared had a train room in which tiny trains traveled through walls and around tree-lined curves; running locomotives with tender cars, cattle, and caboose emerged from tunnels to travel into quaint villages and bustling cities. Entire historic railroad worlds were created in our converted garages and guest rooms.

My railroad education began the week after our wedding and continued through our fifty years of marriage. I learned the difference between a tender and a caboose, the virtues of steam locomotive versus diesel, and the dimensions of the ideal home train room. In turn, I shared my passion for dogs, and my spouse learned about the mischief a single golden retriever could silently pursue on an unsupervised train layout. I accompanied my railroad man to tours, events, and exhibits of model railroads of various scales and themes, where I discovered another surprise.

Railroads and dogs share a common history.

Many miniature model train layouts we visited featured a model of a canine resident or two engaged in mischievous doggy activities in the tiny village or community. Tiny model dogs chased mail carriers, rode on cabooses, and sat in the doorways to welcome home weary travelers; dogs were everywhere on the miniature railroads.

I was impressed and curious about the evolving human partnerships with dogs that I saw memorialized in these model railroad communities

Preface

and the enduring stories of the famous dogs who rode the railroads of America. I discovered a collection of legendary canines who rode the railways and adopted railroads and railroad workers as their home and family. Some stray canines found homes on America's railroads and in railroad communities.

The stories of railway dogs resonated with me. But I wondered: Why would a dog choose life on a railroad? What about these unlikely raildogs that could evoke such a bond between a stray dog and an entire community? Why did the men and women of railroad communities react to these itinerant raildogs in the way they did? Why were the raildog stories so compelling?

My journey to tell and understand the stories of the railway dogs and their relationships with the people of American railroads began. I became a student of canine railroad history.

Dogs of the Railways is about the charismatic vagabond canines who lived life on their own terms on America's railroads and became symbols of the constancy of the human-animal bond and the spirit of America. The themes of this book are the enduring quest for community and belonging, the lure of the rails, and the power of dogs to cut across boundaries of space, culture, and hardship to bring communities together even in difficult times. The book also explores the enduring love and constancy of the human-animal bond and the many ways both dogs and humans define home.

The book has 12 chapters. The first eight chapters include the story of a railway dog, a description and history of the railroad community that embraced the canine vagabond, and an analysis of the legacy of the dog to the community. Chapter 9 discusses raildogs as guardians of today's railroads, and Chapter 10 highlights the events that allowed companion pets to hop on board today's passenger trains. Chapter 11 adds stories of some noteworthy international raildogs who rode the rails. The final chapter explores why dogs rode the rails and why the dogs of the railways became such darlings of railroad communities.

The stories of the raildogs in the chapters are my interpretations based on research and sources that described the dogs and actual historical events. I tried to stay true to the facts or descriptions I discovered in the various source materials that inspired the stories. I learned a considerable amount of information about the breed, lineage, and appearance of some, but not all, dogs. When details were not provided, I offered the dogs' likely descriptions based on their breed characteristics.

I believe our words and terminology matter in how we tell dogs'

Preface

stories. Our language should recognize animals as living beings, not objects. I have attempted to use terms representing dogs as fellow species who share our world and avoid stereotyping them with human-centered terms. I have avoided terminology that refers to dogs as tools, entertainers, or objects, and I have described the dogs by gender (he or she, him or her) rather than calling them "it" since "it" implies an object. I have used the terms *guardian* and *handler* to refer to the human in the human-animal bond rather than *owner* to reflect a human-canine partnership rather than an object relationship. In places where I have referred to *our* dogs, the use of *our* is intended to imply partnership (as in "our partners"), not ownership. I have avoided the term *master* or *mistress* unless I quote a primary source that used that term. Humans share our world with dogs; we are both parts of the animal world. Throughout this book, the term *animal* is used to designate only nonhuman animals but recognizes that humans are part of the animal kingdom.

Some railroad names evolved over time from railroad to railway. I have used the term I felt best reflected the railroad name at the time of the raildog's travels. The author recognizes that some railroad policies may have changed by the time this book is read and encourages the reader to explore the most current information available on these railroads.

Today dogs continue to find their families and communities in many places besides our homes. They discover a family on railroads, on city streets, and in rural towns; in encampments of modern-day homeless persons; and with bands of comrades on the battlefield. This book is written in the hope that it inspires curiosity, learning, and understanding of those unique dogs who choose their own homes and become part of the heart of diverse communities.

Some dogs chose the railroad as home. These are their stories.

Introduction

Climb aboard. Travel the rails with a collection of vagabond canines who lived on their own terms on America's railroads, dogs who became national heroes, and community celebrities. This book tells the true stories of the dogs who traveled and lived on America's railways and became symbols of the independent spirit of America.

As railroads transformed America, dogs were part of the story. Vagabond dogs and railroads intersected at pivotal moments in the trajectory of railroad communities. As the railroads changed the American landscape, railway dogs changed the people who lived and worked in railroad communities. Dogs showed these communities the power of grief and mourning, courage and bravery, and the human and animal need for belonging. They made people laugh when smiles were hard to come by—when danger and sadness were a way of life. A pregnant dog rescued by railroad men during the Great Depression showed a community the enduring power of kindness even in hard times. Itinerant dogs became celebrities, mascots, hometown heroes, and media darlings. Railway dogs gave back to the communities who gave them their homes. They created community pride and spirit and helped with philanthropy and policing rail communities.

The adventures of the railway dogs stretched across decades of industrial and cultural boundaries, vast expanses of American railroads, and into the heart of small towns. Shep, Annie, Roxey, Owney, Railroad Jack, and the other raildogs you are about to meet were errant knights of the rails who evoked images of the changing success and fates of Americans. Dogs who rode the rails or lived within railroad communities represented independence of spirit, loyalty, and the search for home and life on one's own terms. Their stories inspired Americans during challenging economic times and societal change.

Introduction

As dogs were climbing on board trains, railroads were changing American life. In May 1869, a new age of railroading was ushered in with the driving of the golden spike. The construction of the transcontinental railroad brought the two coasts together and enhanced the economic and political future of the United States. Railroads connected previously isolated communities. The railroad extended possibilities. People could change where they lived and worked. Towns along the railways developed and thrived.[1] Smaller railroad companies eventually were absorbed by larger systems.

Along with the challenges of adjusting to changes brought by urbanization and industrialization, Americans were swept along with the developing romance and adventure of the railroads. Railroads were evolving from primarily freight transportation to comfortable transportation with room for sleeping and dining; this dynamic form of travel offered luxurious elegance and innovative technology.

Trains occupied an extraordinary place in the imagination. The lure of the open road, adventures, new beginnings, and the vagabond life conjured up deep emotions in the American psyche. The railroad attracted adventurers, visionaries, dreamers, rogues, and drifters. A canine railway hobo was irresistible. A railroad dog detective like Sheba's Bob with ears that touched the ground was a rock star.

During the industrialization and urbanization of America, people's relationships with animals also changed. Humans began to accept dogs for companionship, not just work, and canines were welcomed into homes and farms. The space a dog inhabited—farm, home, or pasture—defined his type of dog. A stray dog, a familiar sight in most communities, lived somewhere in between, neither domesticated nor wild. With all their charisma and grit, most of the dogs of the railways were still strays. They lacked a geographic home or guardian.

Free-roaming dogs can be considered stray dogs for several reasons. They may have never had human guardians or been abandoned or separated from their homes. Some are feral. Regardless of the source of their homelessness, strays are often shunned by communities and viewed as nuisances, pests, or dangerous canine thugs. The raildogs broke this stereotype and became objects of media attention and even community devotion. The human-animal bond grew between the dog and an entire railroad community.

In this book we ask, why would a stray dog choose life on a train?

Introduction

Each raildog was propelled by his or her own fate and circumstances for becoming a hobo. Dogs were attracted to the tracks for many of the same reasons their human counterparts were. Sometimes their job was on the railroad. For a dog, the railroad environment was appealing; trains felt good. Railroads were filled with clatter and a plentiful assortment of exciting whistles. The comings and goings of trains were predictable. For the most part, they ran on schedule. A raildog could predict the arrival of the daily 5:15 passenger train from the West with the same precision Rover remembers that 5:15 signals dinner time. Schedules matter to dogs.

Life on a train and train stations is lived in small spaces with changing landscapes, and both familiar and unusual smells appeal to dogs. Train journeys encouraged familiarity and casual camaraderie among human and canine travelers interested in sharing tasty food and communication.

We will explore another question. What about these unlikely raildogs could induce such a bond with an entire community? Stories of dogs who lived their life on the rails resonated and evoked strong emotions in people who sought adventure and hope despite their often grim day-to-day reality in a railroad community.

You may be familiar with many of these dogs' stories and meet some of the railway dogs for the first time. Even if this is not your first introduction to the dogs who rode the rails, I hope this book will be the first to show how these independent canines changed and inspired the communities that embraced them and how the raildogs represented a human-animal journey of shared vulnerabilities. While other books have told the stories of individual railway dogs, this book brings together a collection of canine vagabonds who were transformative for railroad communities. It also examines the impact of railroads on America to show how the raildogs and a nation intertwined during decades of change brought about by the railroad.

Dogs of the Railways is the story of the human-canine transformative connections that inspired communities during difficult times. The people of the railroads bonded with itinerant railway dogs as both searched for belonging, community, adventure, safety, and constancy as the world around them changed. The raildogs loved trains, and the railroad community loved the dogs because of it. The train and the railroad became a community—for an hour, a day, or a lifetime. The stray dogs of the railways became a new category: community dogs. Modern

Introduction

raildogs became respected guardians of the railways. Still other rail riding canines were eventually welcomed as fellow travelers with their human companions. For all these dogs of the railways, home became the hearts of the people of the railroad.

Climb aboard. Meet the dogs of the railways.

1

Owney

*Guardian of the Railway
Mail Service, 1888–1897*

He arrived in Maysville, Kentucky, riding on a mailbag on a Saturday night in September 1894. He carried a chest full of medals, an air of mystery, and a hefty load of railroader moxie. The mail car was his home and hearth, and he knew every inch of her. He had discovered her smells, sounds, and daily routines.

He had one blind eye and a sharp, short little nose and was plump from his tendency to enjoy fine dining. No one was sure how old he was, where he came from, or how long he planned to stay. The crowd of thousands who greeted him could only guess at his history. He had traveled the Maysville–Cincinnati train route, dined at breakfast and lunch with mail rail workers, and went on to enjoy a day as an honored guest of the town until he departed the train for Cincinnati, where he spent a week attending the Convention of Postal Clerks. Before leaving Maysville, he was presented with a gold badge from the mail carriers of the main office with the inscription, "Letter carriers Maysville, Ky, September 2, 1894."[1] The charismatic traveler to Maysville that evening was Owney, the mascot dog of the U.S. Railway Service.

* * *

Owney, the guardian of the Railway mail service, would go on to travel more than 140,000 miles in his role as a U.S. Railway Mail Service ambassador.[2]

He became a talisman for luck and was a sentimental part of the rank-and-file railway family. The traveling pup operated from Albany as his home base, but he knew every postal worker in the East, and anyone he passed granted the dog the right of way. No one interfered with him as a special ambassador of the railroad. Owney maintained watch over the

Dogs of the Railways

mail and its workers with a love connection forged on the rails. Owney became a metaphor for good luck, rugged individualism, and the spirit of the railroad men who safeguarded and delivered America's mail.

Several versions exist of the story of how Owney first arrived in Albany, New York, railroad station, where he began his life as a railway dog.[3] Most sources concur that Owney's career as a train hopper canine started in autumn of 1888 when the shaggy mutt wandered into the Albany post office seeking warmth and found a warm, cozy place on a heap of mail sacks. A mail clerk befriended the stray dog and shared his lunch with the pup. Another rail clerk convinced the Albany clerk to let him take Owney on the road, and the dog accompanied the railway man to work. The stray pup charmed the men of the postal rail service, and his new family named him Owney.

As he traveled with his new railman guardian, Owney loved riding near and on the mailbags and became accustomed to their texture and scent. When Owney's adopted guardian moved away, the orphaned pup began following the bags onto the mail wagons and then onto the trains, where he slept. The station and the smell and texture of mailbags felt like home to the itinerant little dog. As Owney rode the daily railway mail car to New York City and back to Albany, he became used to the signature sights of the railroad world, the daily routines, and even the clerks' uniforms and the smells of the well-traveled mailbags.[4] The U.S. Mail Railway Service became his home and family.

The little dog soon expanded his range as he became a regular traveler on the Railway Mail Service. He crossed the country on U.S. mail trains, preferring mail cars to Pullmans or sleepers. He lounged by the door on mailbags and watched the passing landscape.

As a treasured member of the railroad family, the feisty traveler was cared for by the men of the U.S. Postal Service. When he arrived in a town, he followed the mailbags into the local post office. He was a welcome guest and could stay as long as he liked. He was often treated to food or might set out on his own searching for a meal. Sometimes Owney stayed overnight in the town and visited with the mail clerks.[5] It was a good life for a wayward dog and brought him fame and family—for a time.

The little canine vagabond's provenance was the source of speculation and theories. His pedigree was a mystery. Some suggested that he looked like a scotch terrier, although larger and slightly heavier than most of that breed. Most agreed he was homely but argued that he was better than handsome; Owney was charismatic and good-natured. The

1. Owney

unusual-looking pup would charm throngs of admirers with his ability to make himself at home wherever he happened to be, whether in frigid Maine, on the plains of Texas, or on the slopes of the Pacific. His charisma invited a warm welcome wherever he went. The canine adventurer traveled solo yet somehow managed to be well groomed. He was ready to be invited to any event or celebration, especially when refreshments were served. Travelers on the trains considered it a great honor to entertain him on his journeys.

No one could be sure which cities and towns the canine traveler had visited, but some clues helped his admirers piece together his itinerary and adventures. In 1891, the Albany postmaster received a mystery letter about Owney. It was from a postmaster in Quebec. It claimed possession of Owney and demanded a ransom of $2 to return the mascot of the railway. Owney had been in Quebec for two weeks and owed room and board. Owney was redeemed.

It wasn't the first time Owney had to be redeemed. Another time a dime museum in Pittsburgh kidnapped Owney and exhibited him for two months. When a postal clerk learned about Owney's fate, he raised enough money to hire an attorney and rescue Owney. In 1894, Owney crossed the border into the Dakotas, and the Albany postmaster paid $14 to get Owney back home.

On a trip in April 1892, he had headed west to Texas, and when he arrived in New York afterward, he was covered in decorations.[6] In Brooklyn, Owney enjoyed a special lunch from the Clarendon Hotel. He sat next to Superintendent of Mails Lyons, a great fan of Owney. The one-eyed dog with matted hair received distinguished attention from the waiters. Owney walked back to the post office basement and chased the boys who carried the mailbags around the office.[7]

On a visit to Everett, Massachusetts, in 1894, the town's postmaster saw that the honored canine mascot of the railway feasted on "several pounds of bologna," and Owney was awarded a Masonic tag during a fellowship ceremony.[8] Owney had Thanksgiving dinner in 1894 in Providence, Rhode Island, hosted by the postmaster, Henry Gardner. Later reports circulated that the traveling canine hobo was so stuffed with holiday goodies that he could hardly waddle off the rail car when he reached New London, Connecticut.[9]

The *Los Angeles Times*[10] reported that Owney visited Asia, North Africa, and the Middle East. One report claimed that he could boast of passports awarded by the Emperor of Japan and several medals containing the Japanese coat of arms.[11] Another source reported:

Dogs of the Railways

> The terrier "Owney" travels from one end of the country to the other in the postal cars, tagged through, petted, talked to, looked out for, as a brother, almost. But sometimes, no matter what the attention, he suddenly departs for the South, the East, or the West and is not seen again for months.[12]

The furry vagabond had earned a reputation for charming fellow travelers in every city on his travels. He considered it a breach of etiquette if a human friend did not extend a handshake upon meeting the railway ambassador.

But it wasn't just fun and games. Owney had serious business; he guarded the mailbags. Owney served as the self-appointed guardian of the mail and allowed no one other than those dressed in regulation uniform to touch a mail pouch. If you did not wear the uniform of a U.S. mail clerk, you could not handle his precious cargo.[13]

Owney lived a life of adventure on his terms. He was independent and could be a rogue. He went where he wanted when he wanted. The feisty dog made his own rules when embarking on his travels. Newspapers across the United States emphasized Owney's independence and determination to travel where and when he liked. They also acknowledged his affection for his railway family and the mail clerks. His fans found these qualities endearing.

However, even the cleverest adventurer sometimes runs into danger, and Owney was no exception. He disappeared for weeks at a time; at one point, his admirers concluded that Owney must have been involved in a canine mishap or altercation because he had lost one ear. It added to his legend. When Owney disappeared for a time in 1893, his family of rail workers feared the wandering canine was dead. It turned out he had been in an accident in Canada but returned safely home.

Owney was an official permanent resident of the railroad and officially adopted it and the railway family as his family. A family looks out for one another. The postal clerks protected Owney, and they didn't want his adventurous spirit to carry him too far away from home. They presented him with a leather collar and a tag reading "'Owney, Post Office, Albany, New York,' to ensure he found his way home to his Albany base."[14]

Travelers used tags to store or check their baggage. As a tribute to the extent of his travels, postal clerks pinned a note to Owney's collar asking that a bagging tag of leather or metal be attached to his collar to show where he had been. Sometimes fans honored the dog with coins and medals. Businesses used the opportunity for promotion by adding tags that advertised their goods and services. Owney's tags became so numerous that they weighed the dog down, and Postmaster John Wanamaker had a

1. Owney

harness made that could display the tags better while Owney traveled. Fraternal organizations, fire departments, and political campaigns provided tokens to Owney. Awarding tags to Owney's collar at each city where he traveled became such a tradition that soon, his collar jingled with the sound of happy adventures. On his trip to the Pacific Coast through Texas and Mexico, someone added a bright new Mexican silver dollar to his collection of medals and tags. As the tag collection grew, Postmaster General Wanaker presented Owney with a coat to display them and named Owney the official mascot of the U.S. Railway Mail Service. Owney carried with him more than 1,000 medals and tags in his career.[15] His first harness is now on permanent display in the Albany Post Office.

One town honored Owney with a dog license, worried that the free-roaming dog might tangle with the law and find himself in jail if he weren't licensed. One story reported that Owney had been held in a pen in one town until his Albany clerk friends purchased a license for him.[16]

His national fame as a traveler meant that a visit by Owney attracted media attention, and reporters filed stories on Owney's visits. Versions of Owney's adventures varied but most appeared true at least in part. Owney's most famous journey began in August 1895 when he participated in a publicity stunt. The Tacoma, Washington, postmaster sent Owney on a trip around the world as an advertising campaign. Tacoma city boosters, Postmaster Alanson Case, and the railway postal clerks arranged for Owney to board the Northern Pacific steamship *Victoria* bound for China and Japan. Mr. Woods, a purser, accompanied the little dog. Newspapers across the country followed the journey and cheered for the canine traveler. Owney rode with mailbags aboard trains and steamships. After traveling for months throughout Asia, the Middle East, Europe, and the continental United States, he returned to New York City on December 23 in time for the holidays and then went home to Albany.

Postmaster Case added a letter to Owney's belongings that read in part, "He is the pet of 100,000 postal employees of the United States of America."[17] Newspapers across the country covered Owney's return to the United States.[18] Throughout his 113-day trip, Owney was the most famous dog in the world.[19]

Mail Mutt Turns into a Lucky Charm

The mail clerks claimed there was not a clerk in the Railway Mail Service from one end of the country to another who didn't think Owney

Dogs of the Railways

was a personal friend. He knew he was among friends who looked after his comfort and saw that he never lacked an excellent meal. Owney distinguished himself in other ways. When a mailbag fell off the wagon, Owney stayed close to the valuable cargo to protect it—making the pudgy mutt a hero.[20]

How did an ordinary dog gain such fame and recognition, and why did he elicit such affection from the U.S. Post Office clerks? The mail clerks had good reason to love Owney. He was their protector and a symbol of their bonds and adventures. But what about him could evoke such a bond between a stray dog and an entire community? A dog who lived on the rails resonated and spurred strong emotions in people who sought adventure and hope despite their often grim day-to-day reality in a railroad community.

Owney became a symbol of America's quest for adventure and life on one's own terms. When a formerly homeless hobo dog began hopping on trains that carried mail around the United States, he symbolized the adventuresome spirit of railway life. As Owney was exploring and investigating America, the rest of the country was discovering itself. America admired the extent and reach of Owney's travels and his zest for seeing new places and meeting new people. Most people in Owney's generation could only dream of traveling to the places the little canine hobo visited. The *Highland Reporter* noted that Owney had "traveled more miles than some of the wealthiest sightseers."[21]

Owney had selected a perfect time and place when he adopted the Albany station as his home base. This station was abundant with possibilities for a vagabond canine and helped increase his visibility to the rest of the nation. The Albany train station was part of the New York Central Rail System, one of the two largest railroads in the country at that time. The station served as a hub, connecting the greater New York and Boston areas in the East with Midwest cities, including Chicago, St. Louis, Cleveland, Cincinnati, Detroit, and others.[22]

He had arrived at the Albany station in an era when most U.S. mail traveled by train. As a result, his reputation traveled as far as he did. Newspaper accounts of the charismatic pup increased his fame to an even wider audience. People were beginning to travel across the country on the rails, leading to adventures with new places and exciting people. People were gaining time off, and the idea of traveling vacations was catching on.[23]

By the time Owney first wandered into the Albany station, railroads had grown across America and brought opportunities for moving

1. Owney

mail faster to more locations. In 1838, all U.S. railroads were designated as "post roads." As rail systems' ability to move more mail faster than stagecoaches or boats grew, the Post Office's reliance on the rail system expanded. By 1840, railroad lines grew, and 2,818 miles of railroad track had been laid in the U.S. By the beginning of the Civil War, 21 years later, 30,000 miles of track were carrying passengers and mail in the country.[24] In 1840, postal officials began to examine their use of railway lines for carrying mail. Agents removed mail from the pouches, separating items destined for post offices along the train route. It was the first step in evolving the relationship between America's railways and mail.[25] By the 1850s, the Post Office Department spent more money to carry mail by rails than by stagecoaches and steamers combined. Railroads carried over 19 million pieces of mail in 1855. Stagecoaches and steamers together took 23 million pieces.

By the mid-century, American railroads became the future for moving mail across America. The rail system provided communication through a network of interconnecting routes. Decentralization was the magic that made the mail move across the broad American landscape into towns, cities, and remote locations. Workers opened and sorted the mail; they processed sacks as soon as they arrived at a station and dispatched them to the local post office.[26] By the end of the 1890s, the Railway Mail Service carried mail through every state in the contiguous United States. Owney traveled to every one.

The scraggly mutt became a good luck charm for the railroad men. They needed luck. The U.S. railway clerks had a big job and a dangerous one. Life on the rails was fraught with adventure but also danger. Train wrecks were part of the job; from 1890 to 1900, there were more than 6,000 accidents involving trains equipped with mail cars. The mail moved fast. Pouches stuffed with mail were placed on train cars as cargo and rolled on the rails unopened to their destinations.

The job of a railway clerk was demanding. Railway clerks faced unpredictable weather, robberies, wrecks, falls, derailments, and fires as they delivered mail.[27] Life for the clerks was filled with risk.[28]

Several factors contributed to the increase in railroad accidents, injuries, and deaths. The number of trains in service increased, and many operated at faster speeds. As the mail service grew, with distribution extending through more territory, speed became an increasingly important factor. The darkness increased hazards. In the 1890s, railway mail trains often worked at night, with more exchanges made from the moving trains. The railway mail clerks had to contend with fast-moving

Dogs of the Railways

cars. They processed mail on trains in constant motion. Life on the rails could be a dangerous business. Wrecks occurred; scalding water from a steam engine posed significant hazards, and oil lamps and wood stoves might tip over or explode. Gallons of hot water could pour into the railway post office car from a jolted steam-driven engine. A mail clerk could be trapped or injured. Items in the mail car could become hazardous when they tore loose in a wreck. Rail cars were wood, and fire or impact could demolish them. A simple spark could ignite a blazing fire. The wooden framed cars did not protect against flames.

The rail clerks needed a source of inspiration and support amid this danger and hard work, and they formed a lasting bond with each other. The camaraderie extended to Owney as a fellow traveler and guardian of the mail. The little dog became a symbol of good luck for the railroad and the men who rose to perform the often dangerous job of delivering America's mail. No train Owney rode had ever been involved in a wreck.[29] The crew decided that trains were safe when Owney was on board.[30]

At its peak, the U.S. Postal Service employed more than 20,000 railway clerks who worked over 216,000 miles of track. They needed a friend, and animals often stepped forward to offer comfort and companionship. Even cats hopped on board on occasion.

The U.S. Railway Postal Museum website has recorded oral histories of the U.S. mail clerks who rode the rails.[31] These interviews provide a rich source of material for details of the lives of the clerks and other workers who adopted stray animals on the rails. An unexpected encounter with an animal was memorable for railway clerk Joseph E. Beauchemin of Lexington, Massachusetts, who entered the Railway Mail Service in 1950 and worked as a line clerk and foreman until 1980. In an interview, he recalled that his most memorable experience was with a railway animal vagabond—this time a cat. Beauchemin reported a favorite memory featuring an animal who joined him for lunch:

> I got off the train, and I went to have my lunch and sit on a bench not far from the train, and a big cat got on my lap. It looked like a monster cat, and I was eating lunch, and I was petting him. And then when I went to get up, he wouldn't get up, wouldn't get off my lap! They were blowing the whistle for me to get back, and he's digging his nails into me if I move, you know, and he finally got off.[32]

At one point, he stopped and pointed out that, on the train, you had to be careful about the soot from the engine when you were on the second car back. On a trip to Waitsfield, he remembered how the crews

1. Owney

were going through town, and the clerk had to "catch and throw"—catch the bag without stopping. If the clerk didn't get it back fast enough, he would "lose the bar," and "the bar would get hit in the building and take it right off."[33]

The challenges of a railroad clerk were unique. Beauchemin grinned as he recalled: "You threw the bags off. You had to be careful you didn't hit the people waiting to get on the train."[34]

For the clerks, their railway comrades became family—even if that comrade had four legs and was a one-eyed pooch. But like railroad men, raildogs got older and their vagabond life could take its toll. For an aging dog, sadly, the love of family could wane.

End of the Line

By the time Owney returned home from his international trip, he had traveled the rails for over eight years and probably was anywhere from 8 to 17 years old. (His actual age was unknown.) After his trip around the world, he was more in demand than ever, and postmasters across the United States requested his attendance at events. Owney had secured a place on the mailbags and in the heart of America even as he aged. But not everyone was a fan.

By early 1897, the once robust and chubby dog looked thin and tired and was not seen by some as the same friendly and outgoing pup he had once been. After a long traveling career, Owney's health deteriorated, and he often had trouble moving. As Owney aged, the Post Office management eventually determined that Owney had become too old and ill to continue his travels.

Owney still often traveled from Albany to Toledo, but his journey left him tired and out of sorts, according to sources.[35] A mail clerk took him in, and a mandate from the Chicago management of the Railway Mail Service asked his employees not to allow Owney on future mail trains. Owney was still popular with the rail workers who loved to visit with the traveling dog, but the superintendent did not want the dog to take up employees' time at the station and declared that Owney was no longer welcome at the rail stations. The mascot of the Railway Mail Service was no longer welcome on his beloved mail cars, at least as far as management was concerned. This decision was not well received by newspapers across the country, who sided with Owney and his railway clerk family.[36]

Dogs of the Railways

The final sequence of the events resulting in Owney's death occurred on June 11, 1897, when Owney traveled to Toledo. Precisely what transpired was the source of speculation, and varying reports surfaced of what took place. One source reported that a postal clerk had arranged for a photographer to shoot a story of Owney when the dog arrived in Toledo Union Station, and had chained Owney up. Then he awaited the photographer's arrival. Not used to being so constrained, the freedom-loving dog began barking protests. The clerk attempted to quiet the noisy canine, and Owney bit him. One report was that Owney followed his regular routines and followed the postmaster into his office, where the postmaster greeted him. The clerks also wanted to say hello. In his later years, Owney had become reluctant at times to let people examine his tags, and this day he reacted with a bite to the mail clerk as the clerk reached for Owney's tag. The Toledo postmaster, hearing the report, summoned a police officer to the scene who shot the mascot of the mail service dead in the street. Some sources reported that when Deputy U.S. Marshal Shannon arrived, Owney tried to attack him, and it was the U.S. marshal who fired the single shot that killed the beloved dog.[37] One newspaper reported that "Owney received the death sentence."[38]

The events that followed Owney's death illustrated the chasm between the workplace attitudes of postal clerks and management. His death highlighted differences in focus and philosophy. The beloved dog provided camaraderie and partnership with the workers, while management theories emphasized efficiency and strict adherence to policies and time management. It was a stressful time for the railroad and its workers. A wandering dog who encouraged affectionate periods of interaction with clerks was incongruent with the model of efficiency. At the same time, the relief and comfort an animal brought to the stressful and dangerous life of the mail clerk had become, for the clerks, a treasured part of the work environment.

Return to Station

Owney's death became a rallying cry. In the summer of 1897, newspapers across the country ran his obituary. People across the United States and the world eulogized the mutt who had led such an extraordinary life.

Postal clerks used Owney's death to make a point. They used to bury their beloved mascot clerks across the country and asked that

1. Owney

Owney receive the honor he was due.[39] In 1904, Owney's effigy was displayed at the St. Louis World's Fair. Postal workers in Cleveland, Ohio, commissioned a commemorative silver spoon.[40] Owney was preserved and taken to the U.S. Post Office headquarters in Washington, D.C., in 1911 and later transferred to the Smithsonian Postal Museum, where he resides today. In 2011, Owney was honored with a U.S. Postal Service Owney Forever stamp, and a new exhibit was designed to celebrate his adventures. In 2011, the Smithsonian Postal Museum and the Humane Society of Southern Arizona hosted an Owney look-alike contest. Owney enjoys a growing fan base today, with a Facebook page listing him as a "public figure" with over 3,000 followers.[41] An online interactive site at the U.S. Postal Museum includes ways for young fans to explore his travels, tags, and newspaper articles to encourage students, teachers, families, and fans to connect with his adventures.

Owney's life and death illustrate the complexity of human-animal relationships and the roles of dogs as symbols, metaphors, and "little humans." Owney was often referred to as the little traveler or ascribed human emotions or feelings. However, when his ability to function as an amusing and stereotypical good buddy ended, he was subject to the unfortunate tendency of some humans to treat dogs as objects rather than like nonhuman animals. When Owney became inconvenient and old, he became disposable. The story of Owney, the mascot of the Railway Mail Service, ended with his being shot dead in the street.

Owney's sad ending is a cautionary tale. Not everyone understands that aging dogs might need special consideration and care, which might mean a less stressful setting. Owney's railroad guardians perhaps did not understand the need to help an aging dog find a comfortable, safe, and calm routine environment in which to spend his golden years.

Humans' feelings about dogs are often ambiguous. Dogs are seen as symbols of love and faithfulness, loyalty, and affection. At the same time, they can be seen as fierce, protective, and dangerous. Dogs endear themselves to us because of their human qualities, and we treat them like family. Owney relied on a human family and chose the railway workers who welcomed him. But even in the best of families, when circumstances change, our canine friends can be seen as dispensable when they exhibit less endearing behaviors and become aged or inconvenient. Too often dogs are surrendered or euthanized because they have become too old, too in need of care, less playful, or less attractive, or because the family no longer needs a canine child when they expect the arrival of a new baby. A former companion animal may now be

Dogs of the Railways

perceived as a potential danger to a child or too great a burden of time or energy. Even our language illustrates this ambiguity. We call someone a dog or an angry bitch and at the same time talk about an endearing puppy or puppy dog eyes.

So our question remains. What attracted this stray dog to a railroad? Owney was drawn to the tracks for many of the same reasons as his human counterparts. The railroad environment was appealing; trains felt good to a homeless dog, and the smells reminded him of his first guardian, who symbolized home. Trains were interesting. Railroads were filled with clatter, people and places, and predictability. Life on a train involved living in small spaces, with changing landscapes and familiar and unusual smells.

Owney sought out a community of people where he felt supported, safe, and even understood. A sense of belonging to a family or tribe is one we humans experience. For us, it means acceptance, companionship, and often safety. We may find a sense of belonging in family, friends, religious groups, and even social media. Like Owney and the rail workers found, belonging to a greater community means connection to others and provides an understanding that we are not alone as we struggle through difficult times.

Owney with his medals, 1885–1897. On exhibit at National Postal Museum, Smithsonian Institution, Curatorial Photographic Collection.

1. Owney

Another attraction is the journey and exploring that opened him to connections he might not have otherwise found. He met like-minded common travelers when he chose the mail clerks as his family. For Owney, every day was a journey—to adventure, belonging, and home.

As Owney's glory days of riding with the mail by rail were drawing to a close, so was the peak era of mail by rail. The railroad industry was changing; through the 1920s and 1930s, the Railway Mail Service realized its greatest reach and strength. Ten thousand or more trains carried mail-sorting clerks across the country in 1930 alone.[42] In the mid–1930s, railway passenger service began a long, steady decline at the height of the Railway Mail Service's success.[43] Post office clerks worked on sorting mail through the Great Depression when mail remained the primary communication method for most Americans; some had taken their jobs as railway clerks after returning from the war. The Railway Mail Service continued to fade in the 1960s and 1970s. Airplanes and trucks carried more and more mail, and the service was renamed the Postal Transportation Service. The Railway Mail Service made its last run on June 30, 1977, when the last railway post office car rolled into Washington, DC's Union Station from New York City.[44]

2

The Railroad Jacks

Hoboes, Travelers, and Philanthropists, Mid–1880s–1931

From the late 19th to the early 20th century, another group of train-hopping dogs captured the attention of an admiring public. By coincidence or design, many of these traveling canines acquired the name Jack. Interest in the railroad Jacks was fueled by American and British magazines and newspapers eager to report on their canine adventures. Stories of vagabond raildogs named Jack spread from England to the United States. They thrilled an admiring public with their extraordinary exploits and escapes from mayhem. They were American and British dogs of different colors, sizes, and breeds. They pursued unique career paths and callings but had more than a name in common. They all found a family on the railroad.

* * *

Railroad Jack of Albany: The "King of the Deadheads," Mid–1880s–1893

While Owney was bouncing across the United States on mailbags, another canine train hopper appeared on the scene in the mid–1880s. Although he did not achieve the rock star status of Owney, Railroad Jack had an enthusiastic public clamoring for news about his exploits. While his contemporary Owney perched on mailbags for his travels, Railroad Jack of Albany preferred a ride in the trains' baggage. Like Owney, Jack was fond of anyone who wore the railroad uniform.

Railroad Jack came on the railroad scene when a New York

2. The Railroad Jacks

Express wagon driver brought his Scotch terrier puppy to Union Station. The pup became fond of the rail staff. They named him Railroad Jack and decked him out with a collar that read, "Property of headquarters at Union Depot Albany, NY." The railroad men introduced the pup to life on the rails and sent him on excursions to area rail stations. The railway crew offered food, drink, and friendship, which the rookie raildog happily accepted. Throughout his rail riding adventures, Railroad Jack was cared for by the railroad men. He became a canine celebrity and was reported to have even attended the inauguration of Grover Cleveland in 1885.[1] Railroad Jack hopped on the baggage cars on almost every line of the railroad in the Eastern United States. He often traveled to Boston and New York and never missed catching the correct train.[2] Jack's favorite excursion was reported to be from Albany to Binghamton[3] and a round trip between Albany and Manhattan.

Jack was started on his journey by Station Master John Kelly. Kelly remembered Jack with pride:

> He was the most knowing animal I ever saw. He would jump into a baggage car and ride to Saratoga. He would stay around Saratoga for a time and then take a train to Round Lake, where he would stay over Sunday, returning here on Monday morning. Next he would be on the train running to Albany, where he would board a West Shore train and ride to Weehawken. He would cross on the ferry to New York and go to Grand Central Station, where he would jump into the luggage car of a New York Central train bound for Albany. He never missed getting on the right train.[4]

Railroad Jack, like Owney, visited Canada and spent time in Montreal, a straight shot on the rails from Albany. When adventurers travel, they often meet the unexpected. When Jack went on tour to the Pacific Coast in 1892, the Union Station men at Albany received a dispatch coming from San Francisco:

> To the Starter of Railroad Jack—
> Dear Sir.
> "Railroad Jack" arrived here last night in B. and O., one of his legs being bruised the result of a "lovers quarrel" at Salt Lake. But after a good supper and a night's rest, he is much better this morning. He will leave here this afternoon or tomorrow. He is a great favorite on the coast and was interviewed by the press representative today.
> Yours etc.
> O.H. Dpt., W.F. and Co., S.F.
> July 18[5]

Dogs of the Railways

As his fame increased, Railroad Jack became a victim to the downside of celebrity. In the summer of 1892, Jack went on a long cross-country train trip from Maine to California and Mexico and returned weighted down with medals and trinkets, including Bowie knives, tomahawks, and skulls. Jack was kidnapped and exhibited in Boston, Montreal, and Toronto along the journey.[6]

The *Ogdensburg Journal* reported on October 17, 1891, "Railroad Jack Stolen"[7]; another newspaper ran the headline "Railroad Jack Kidnapped."[8] According to the story, Railroad Jack left Troy six weeks before, and his whereabouts were unknown until a clue finally appeared on October 16, when an article in the *New York Herald* reported that Jack had died in Buffalo. The railroad men had grown attached to Jack and were upset to think Jack may have died. That was until a group of railroad men in Buffalo sent their Troy colleagues a surprising newspaper article. The message from Buffalo included an advertisement for a museum in Buffalo that advertised that "Railroad Jack, the tramp dog" was on display along with other unusual exhibits. The Buffalo railroad men reported that Railroad Jack was being held captive by a freak show showman who had captured Jack in Buffalo. Outraged at their canine friend's captivity and humiliation, the Troy railroad men devised a plan to rescue Jack. An agreement was made with the perpetrator, who agreed to release Jack.[9]

In 1892, Railroad Jack made his last public appearance in style. Albany celebrated Columbus Day with a parade featuring local Italian societies and scenic floats, including seven military divisions. The floats were decorated with various themes, but one that attracted much attention was the float of the local New York Central employees.[10]

Lanterns adorned the float, and Jack perched on a pedestal in front of two headlights of a pair of enormous locomotives. The oldest bell from New York Central was displayed above him. Jack's trunk sat in front of him and was packed with the souvenirs he acquired on this last transcontinental trip. On the side was the inscription:

> Railroad Jack, mascot of the Empire State Express, home again. Traveler from the Atlantic to the Pacific, from the Gulf of Mexico to the Atlantic Ocean: he never pays fare. King of the Deadheads.
> I have traveled more miles and over more railroads than Nellie Bly.—*Railroad Jack*

By early 1893, Jack's train-hopping days were over. With years of traveling and adventures behind him, he had grown old and put on

2. The Railroad Jacks

pounds due to his many treats and meals on the road. He spent his retirement days roaming the union depot's baggage room.

When Jack died in 1893, he was estimated to be 19 years old. Newspapers across the country reported that Railroad Jack had died and that his remains were to be stuffed. The *New York Times* ran Jack's obituary on June 16, 1893,[11] announcing, "Railroad Jack, one of Albany's two noted railroad dogs, is dead."[12] The *Times* reported some details of his death—that Jack died suddenly after eating some type of food and that he walked to the baggage room, looked at the moving cars and engines for a short time, and then fell dead on the floor.[13]

Railroad Jack's obituary briefly mentioned the newcomer, Albany Railway Dog Owney. The *Times* obituary noted that the only dog Railroad Jack ever took note of was Owney, the Albany Post Office dog,[14] pointing out that while Owney rode the mailbags, Railroad Jack was strictly a baggage car dog. After 13 years of active life, in which he had earned an honorable reputation in all parts of the United States, Jack had traveled more miles on the railway than any other dog.

The final location of Railroad Jack remains unclear. Reports were that, like Owney, Railroad Jack was taxidermized and was in a case at Albany's Union Station for a time on Broadway. When the Schenectady Station wanted him, Jack's stuffed body traveled there. The last known resting place of Railroad Jack was an animal display in a North Pearl Street store window.[15]

The *Poughkeepsie Evening Enterprise*, on July 26, 1897, reported that after the original Jack died, the railroad men at Albany got another dog and promptly named him Railroad Jack. That Jack's career as a railway dog was short-lived. He was playing on the tracks one night, and the engine of the first mail train ran over him.[16]

Northwestern Pacific Railroad: Boomer Jack the Logging Hobo, 1914–1926

The Northwestern Pacific Railroad (NWP) boasted of an independent black dog who adopted the NWP as his home. Boomer Jack first appeared around 1914 and rode NWP trains from Trinidad to Sausalito for 14 years until he died in 1926. He was cared for by the NWP family. Boomer Jack was like the railroad logging men he loved, best known for his independent spirit and love of freedom. He was a free-spirit, rugged railroad hobo. He rode the rails when and where the spirit called him;

he rode the Eureka streetcars and knew the houses of the railroad men. He was cared for by the railroad men who would stay in a town for a day or two and then move on.

NWP was built as a logging railroad vital to Northern California's development. Six railroad companies held by the Santa Fe and Southern Pacific railroads consolidated in 1907 to form the NWP. Rail service to inland areas facilitated the local development of the lumber industry. Eventually, the NWP became the consolidation of 60 other railroad companies, some with logging lines and other companies with no rail lines. The NWP became a wholly owned subsidiary of Southern Pacific when it bought Santa Fe's interest in the line and has remained a wholly owned subsidiary ever since. In 1929, the Atchison, Topeka, and Santa Fe Railway sold its half-interest to the Southern Pacific, making the NWP a full Southern Pacific subsidiary.[17]

Jack often went to San Francisco on the NWP ferries. The railroad used ferries across San Francisco Bay to transfer freight and connect to the national rail network at Napa Junction by the Santa Rosa and Carquinez Railroad. Boomer Jack even stayed in a San Francisco hotel, having been secretly let in by a railroad man. After he was ejected, the feisty canine returned and left a calling card by lifting his leg at the hotel.

Boomer Jack once made a wrong connection and landed in South Carolina. Jack's friends worried about him and feared he was lost. The NWP home office received a telegram that a dog with an NWP badge on his collar had been found. They rushed to wire his finders instructions on returning their canine colleague, and Boomer Jack was returned safely to his home line.

Boomer Jack had to be as tough as the rugged men of the logging community. Riding trains was dangerous for men and dogs. When the raildog fell from a train and suffered a severe leg injury, his admirers and friends established a fund to pay his medical bills and a bank account in his name. Jack's leg slowed him down, and now he needed help getting into a cab. Boomer Jack died in 1926. He was found lying on the ground in front of the Willits station and was buried in a small wooden coffin in the Willits switchyard.[18]

In 2013, Timothy Martin wrote a fictionalized book based on Boomer Jack. *Somewhere Down the Line: The Legend of Boomer Jack* is based on a story of a dog who rode the lumber trains of Northern California in the early 1900s.[19] Lincoln Kilian wrote a book about Boomer Jack published by the Mendocino County Museum, *A Dog's Life: Boomer*

Jack of the Northwestern Pacific. Kilian, a historian at Humboldt State University, researched the life of Boomer Jack and discovered he was a legendary hobo dog. He interviewed Northern California train workers who were old enough to have memories of Boomer Jack and his story. Kilian wrote his book in 1998, and it was sold at the museum bookstore and eventually other outlets.[20]

Railway Jack of Lewes Station: The English Traveler, 1879–1890

Railway Jack of Lewes Station was a fox terrier based in Sussex, England, who traveled on the London, Brighton, and South Coast railway trains in England from 1879 to 1890. There's some debate about the breed of Railway Jack, but some illustrations show him as a dog similar to a fox terrier. He was white, black, brown, and big.

He lived at the Lewes railway station but made daily trips to Portsmouth, Horsham, or Brighton. He always caught the last train back to Lewes to sleep. In November 1880, when he spent a whole week away from Lewes, a Scottish railway guard knew the friendly dog and fed and housed him before Jack returned to Lewes. Railway Jack arrived in Brighton by train into Steyning, got off the train briefly, and went on the same train to Henfield, where he went to a public house and feasted on a biscuit. He then caught the last train back to West Grinstead, where he spent the afternoon before returning to Brighton in time for the last train to Lewes.[21]

Jack went about on his own and had friends everywhere on the railway. In 1880, the railway men presented Jack with a silver collar inscribed "Jack, London B and S Coast Railway Company."[22]

A true adventurer, Jack went wherever he wished to go, whenever he wanted to go, and could jump on any train that suited him. No amount of coaxing could invite Jack to change his mind once he decided to stay or change cars. A military officer who claimed to have known Jack for four years said that the traveling dog knew the London Bridge and Victoria stations as well as he did.[23] Jack even traveled to Paris.

He developed a following of fans who journeyed to Lewes to see the traveling dog. With a tip to the stationmaster, they might be allowed to feed Jack and watch him hop the next train.

Mrs. Knight, the wife of one of the London, Brighton, and South

Dogs of the Railways

Coast Railway managers, presented Jack with a new collar. The collar read, "I am Jack the L.B. & S.C. Railway dog—please give me a drink and I will then go home to Lewes." After this, Jack took a shine to Mrs. Knight and would often stay over and enjoy breakfast with the family before accompanying Mr. Knight to the station to return home to Lewes.[24]

Jack occasionally visited Eastbourne, where he would wander across the road to get a drink and food at the Gildredge Hotel on Terminus Road.[25] A reporter tracked Jack on one of his trips. Jack took the morning train to Brighton and went on to Portsmouth, where he enjoyed his lunch. He then moved on to Littlehampton, where a photographer captured the trip at No. 21 High Street.[26]

On one of his adventures, Jack barely escaped death by falling under an oncoming train while pursuing a dead bird at Northwood Junction. Jack's left paw was injured and had to be amputated by a veterinary surgeon back at Lewes. Jack was cared for by the veterinary surgeon's wife, and the railroad clerks took turns holding vigil while the beloved dog recovered. The resilient pooch soon learned to walk on three legs. His celebrity increased after his injury.[27]

Railway Jack hosted several dignitaries. Judge Sir Henry Hawkins came to Lewes on July 18, 1882, and visited Railway Jack. Hawkins was known as the hanging judge but was very fond of dogs. The judge saw Jack board the Brighton train and sent Jack a collar mounted in silver with the inscription, "I am Railway Jack—treat me well and send me home to the station master at Lewes. Presented by Sir Henry Hawkins to Jack, July 18, 1882."[28]

After his accident, Jack's schedule and life slowed down. Although his life as a traveling dog was over, Railway Jack had become a companion dog, living with his railroad friend, Mr. Moore—both of them retired veterans of the rails. However, through the 1880s, Mr. Moore and Railway Jack were still minor celebrities, so in their retirements, they were often invited as guests at dog owners' shows and railway conventions and made trips together as the guests of railway companies. The three-legged dog sat on Moore's lap, eagerly watching the trains and locomotives when they reached the station. Jack had three silver presentation collars and a large silver medal. On October 18, 1890, Railway Jack made his last journey and died of old age in the arms of Mr. Moore. He was said to be 13 years old.

In the 1880s and 1890s, several other Railway Jack traveling dogs emerged who tried to emulate Jack's exploits. Still, none of these train-hoppers achieved his notoriety or success at covering distance on the rails. However, one raildog named Jack emerged to capture the dog-loving public's attention with his charitable mission. Charity London Jack started a dog dynasty of railway collecting dogs, all named Jack.

The Charity London Jacks: A Philanthropic Dynasty, 1894–1931

Charity London Jack was a famous black Labrador who lived a railroad life patrolling London Waterloo station as one of Britain's collecting dogs. He was not a train hopper but had a home base. London Jack was one of many dogs who collected money for charity, patrolling London's Waterloo Railway Station and often other railroad stations throughout Britain.[29] He started the line of collecting dogs named London Jack.

London Jack collected at Waterloo station for the Southern Railway Orphanage at Woking. Jack was born in 1917 and started collecting in 1923. Jack retired in 1930 and died in 1931. By that time, he had collected over 4500 pounds for the orphanage.[30] London Jack was not alone in his collecting duties; he was one of four collecting dogs, but Jack was the canine star of the collectors. He became a London celebrity, and newspapers and an admiring public followed his adventures.

From the mid–Victorian era to the 1950s, raildogs collected donations for charity at British train stations. Railroads and hospitals used the collecting dogs, who collected thousands of pounds for railroad charities. They carried a sign and a collecting box. They encouraged people to put contributions in the box for charity. They sometimes boarded trains on their own, mixed with the train travelers, and performed tricks for donations.[31] Most charity dogs were allowed to walk loose around the railway station, although some worked on a leash.

The railway family needed the raildogs' support in Britain as in America. In the 1880s, life on the rails was hazardous, and the railroad workers and their families needed a charity to support injured railway men or their widows and children. If a child's father was killed or hurt, no welfare state existed to care for the children, and the orphanage filled this need. The London and South Western Railway Servants'

Dogs of the Railways

Orphanage was founded as a home for "fatherless girls" but was later expanded to include "fatherless boys." The orphanage moved to Woking in 1909 and, by the 1930s, cared for 200 children. The name was changed in 1923 to the Southern Railway Servants' Orphanage and later to the Southern Railwaymen's Home for Children. Woking Homes, as it is now known, still provides care and living accommodations for retired rail workers.[32]

Collecting dogs became a novelty and were more appealing and popular than human fundraisers. They had more luck than their human counterparts in raising much-needed dollars to support the rail family. The British press followed the railway dogs and reported their exploits and adventures. The public was eager to read about the fortunes of the collecting dogs and reports on their welfare. They had affection for the dogs and were concerned for them while at the same time eager to hear about the collecting dogs' adventures, and Charity Jack had his share.

Charity London Jack disappeared in 1899. His trainer, Mr. Wickins, a railway man, worried that his star collecting dog was being held for ransom. Jack's public was outraged and concerned that their canine philanthropist may have met a bad fate. Various stray Labradors were sent to Waterloo, but none proved to be Jack. In September, a young man gave a tip to authorities after hearing barking day and night. The neighborhood had been the scene of recent dog thefts, and mysterious men had come and gone at all hours of the night. The constable and his team raided the premise and found Jack among 62 other kidnapped dogs. Jack was very thin and nervous after his ordeal. Jack never resumed his previous health and vigor and retired in 1900 to the Isle of Wight, where he was cared for by an old railway man.

The public and Mr. Wickins had good reason to be concerned for Jack's welfare. The collecting dogs' proceeds were tempting to nefarious sorts, and the collecting dogs were often the victims of thieves after the contributions placed in the dogs' boxes.

In 1896, a gang of criminals had assaulted Tim, an Irish terrier working at London's Paddington station. The perpetrators held Tim upside down over a suitcase and shook him until the coins from his collections fell out. But Tim defended his loot. He bit one of the assailants on the leg.

A few collecting dogs strayed from the straight and narrow themselves. It was reported that Brighton Bob, a collecting dog in the 1860s,

2. The Railroad Jacks

had used some of his money to buy biscuits at a bakery and was caught in the act by a reporter.[33]

The canine philanthropists were often stuffed after their death and put on display at a station so they could continue collecting for the charity. When Charity London Jack died, he was stuffed and displayed in a cabinet. The public could donate coins through a slot in the front of the cabinet. Jack continued his good works after his death. A plaque in front of his case at the Bluebell Railroad Museum reads: "Though dead, Jack is still on duty and solicits a continuance of your contributions in support of his good work for the orphans."[34]

Charity London Jack launched a raildog dynasty of canine philanthropists. An entire line of London Jacks served the railway, with the first serving in 1894. Before he retired, London Jack was bred to a half-breed Newfoundland, and London Jack 2 took his place as heir to his father's tradition as a second-generation collecting dog at Waterloo Platform. Jack 2 always stopped to greet his father's stuffed body in a glass case. In 1905, a newspaper article described Jack 2 as the most famous collecting dog in the world. He received an award of a handsome silver collar with silver medals, each representing 100 pounds collected for the orphans. Jack also broke up an occasional fight among the inebriated of London. In June 1907, Jack 2 died from cancer.

Jack 2's son, London Jack 3, followed the family tradition and took up the collecting family business. Jack 3 resembled a black Labrador and lived to a ripe old age. A fourth London Jack was active throughout the 1920s and continued working even with failing eyesight until he was ten years old. Most London Jacks ultimately met with the taxidermist and kept collecting after their death.

Jack 5 was born in 1917 and began collecting in 1923. His contributions benefited an orphanage for railway men's children in Surrey. He wore a collection of medals on his neck, signifying every 100 pounds he raised, with a gold one for every 500. In 1924, he was photographed with actor Jackie Coogan who starred in the film *The Kid*. In 1930, Jack 5's eyesight diminished, and he retired. He died the following year and was stuffed and mounted in a cabinet. He traveled from Waterloo to the Bluebell Railway, where he was to have his final resting place. On his way to his resting spot, he changed color, and for many successive years, he was identified as a golden rather than a black retriever. Colin Tyson, the editor of the *Bluebell Railway* newsletter, said, "He was in the case for a number of years and must have become bleached by the light over time."[35] Jack 5 went for a restoration and was dyed black again when the taxidermist discovered that the blonde Jack 5 had black roots.[36] With Jack 5, the remarkable London Jack dynasty of collecting dogs ended.

The number of station dogs had dwindled by the time Britain's trains were nationalized in 1948. The corporate heads of the British railroads removed the stuffed dogs, reluctant to have things like dead dogs in the station. But collecting dogs like Railroad Jack were an important part of British railroad heritage and helped many causes.[37]

New Opportunities for Today's Railroad Jacks

From the 1800s to the mid–20th century, times were good for a traveling railroad canine hobo. One of the reasons they chose a life on the railways was positive reinforcement.[38] Adventure and welcoming communities beckoned them. But modern-day raildogs are confronted with different challenges and opportunities to partner with a human rail family. Trains developed more rigorous regulations. Platforms today must be carefully guarded. In Chapters 9 and 10, we will see modern-day raildogs partner with humans to keep rail passengers and employees safe from the new hazards they face.

3

Roxey

The Long Island Railroad Commuter, 1904–1914

The train steamed onto Oyster Bay, and the yellow dog sauntered into the private car on the Long Island Railroad (LIRR) and curled up on the bed. Someone had furnished the car in high style, and this bed was the perfect spot for a raildog's snooze. This bed needed to be comfortable. It was made up for a presidential nap.

This particular car on the LIRR train was none other than the presidential car of President Theodore Roosevelt. Roxey had hopped on a private car taking President Roosevelt to Sagamore, his summer home on Oyster Bay. When a porter discovered Roxey snoozing away on the bed, he approached the stowaway dog to eject him from the bed and the car. But then the conductor pointed to the dog's collar. The sleeping pup wore a nickel-plated collar with a silver plate inscribed, "I am Roxey, the LIRR dog. Whose dog are you?"[1]

Roxey held a special LIRR rail pass and was granted free napping privileges. Ralph Peters, president of the LIRR, had awarded Roxey an unlimited pass made of metal and affixed it to Roxey's collar. The pass granted the traveling dog unlimited access to ride the LIRR with an order that required any passenger or employee to give Roxey a seat, even in the parlor car. It entitled him to ride any train at any time. All branches of the LIRR were required to accept Roxey's lifetime pass. The conductor would announce, "President Peters' orders are that Roxey has the privilege to occupy a seat in any car at all times."[2]

Railroad rules applied to presidents, too. So when the raildog curled up on the president's bed and Roosevelt arrived and heard Roxey's story, the commander-in-chief insisted that Roxey ride with him the rest of the train trip. Roxey rode and napped on the journey with his presidential friend.

Dogs of the Railways

Theodore Roosevelt was no stranger to the LIRR; he depended on it for his Rough Riders' cavalry to travel to Camp Wyckoff in Montauk Hills, where they were quarantined. When he established a training unit for the cavalry at Amagansett, the LIRR transported men and equipment. When the Rough Riders returned triumphant from Cuba, Roosevelt had become a national hero. He made an LIRR tour of Long Island, wearing his uniform and a broad-brimmed hat, as he waved to cheering crowds from the rear platform of Superintendent Potter's private car. It's not every pooch that becomes a traveling companion of a president.

* * *

Roxey was a goodwill ambassador for an entire railroad, a friend and mascot for the LIRR, and a lifetime member of the YMCA. Roxey was part of the heart and soul of the people of the LIRR.[3] But how did a dog become a goodwill ambassador on the busy LIRR and come to be memorialized and honored with a gravestone at the Merrick train station?

What brought him to the LIRR one rainy night is the source of considerable conjecture. Multiple theories on his origin are part of Roxey's mystique, and the mystery endures. Most authorities agree that Roxey began life as a stray street dog, a homeless pup wandering in search of home and kindness. One theory is that the mongrel pup arrived on the LIRR in 1901 when he met Mrs. Ellphat Willets of Roslyn, Long Island, at First Avenue and 34th Street. The puppy followed her to the Long Island Ferry. Mrs. Willets thought she might adopt the friendly pup, and as she got on the train for Roslyn, she asked the baggage man to put the dog off with her when they arrived at her destination. Roxey jumped off in Floral Park, where an LIRR conductor met him. A mix-up occurred, and Roxey and his potential adopter were never reunited when the train pulled into their destination.

Another version of Roxey's first appearance on the LIRR is that Roxey just appeared at the rail yard at the Garden City station when he was frightened during a summer thunderstorm.[4] The stationmaster, Agent Heaney, adopted Roxey. The pup's passion for train hopping took him away from the station, and he traveled by train all over Long Island. Roxey broke some railroad rules but gained admirers and friends wherever he traveled. Luckily, the LIRR's president, Ralph Peters, had a heart for the wandering dog.

The *South Side Signal* newspaper reported a version of how Roxey became the pet of the LIRR and termed Roxey a "New York waif." The

3. Roxey

wayward pup charmed a well-dressed woman to consider adopting him and boarded the train with her. The woman changed her mind and asked the railroad men to care for the homeless pup.[5]

Still, another story of Roxey's arrival describes a scenario in which a young lady hurrying to catch the 34th Street ferry in New York noticed the forlorn pup and patted Roxey on the head.[6] with that, Roxey sprang into action and followed the friendly young woman onto the train. He slept under the seat during the train ride but didn't wake up when she disembarked at Garden City. When he did leave the train coach, a storm was brewing, so the little dog sought refuge at the side of the station. As the storm raged on, Roxey became more insistent about gaining entry to the station. He barked loud enough to alert the stationmaster, who discovered the wayward waif of a pup and let him in. A railroad agent took the dog home, adopted him, and named him Roxey, after one of his beloved pets.[7] He thought Roxey would make a perfect railroad station dog, and he proved correct.

All the stories of his arrival agree on a few details of Roxey's adoption. The LIRR stationmaster adopted him and named the pup Roxey (also spelled Roxie and Roxy) after a dog he had once owned. The orphaned pup was never reunited with his female companion but grew into a medium-sized adult yellow dog and found home and family on the LIRR.

However he came to arrive at the railroad, it is undisputed that Roxey enjoyed a lifetime of the kindness of the rail employees and made his home on the rails. He took an immediate liking to railroad men, baggage cars, cabooses, locomotives, and anyone who wore the uniform of the LIRR. The railroad men and the LIRR community returned the affection and taught their new friend tricks. But Roxey's best tricks became his daily rounds on the railroad.

A Canine Commuter on the LIRR

For the next 12 years, Roxey rode the LIRR each day. He loved hopping trains, and he never missed a connection. Each day the yellow dog traveled the rails of the LIRR and visited towns and stations along the route. He spent his days cruising Long Island by rail and nights in Garden City with Mr. Keenan, the railroad agent. Roxey's home station was in Long Island City. The railroad family nicknamed him "the commuter," but he never responded to any name but Roxey.[8] Roxey was described as "a

Dogs of the Railways

good traveling man and a conscientious advertiser for the railroad"[9]; the railroad men gave the little stray dog a chance at life—a life on the rails.

Roxey learned how to be a raildog and travel smoothly. He would often be seen sidestepping down the railroad car aisle as the rails' motion temporarily halted his progress.[10] Like most dogs, Roxey had his favorite places. He loved riding the train's engine best, preferring the fireman's seat. For a small orphaned dog, looking out the window of the moving train must have seemed like traveling a tremendous moving river of track, an endless adventure with a group of like-minded comrades.

In 1911, *The New York Times* dubbed Roxey "a dog with many masters,"[11] noting that Roxey was loyal to one and all LIRR men. The *Times* reported that Roxey would change cars in Jamaica and take the Brooklyn Express. One day someone diverted him through Penn Station to New York, where he enjoyed a turkey dinner.

> A funny thing about Roxy's friendships is that while at the Pennsylvania Station, he is polite to everybody; he reserves familiarities for Long Island Railroad men, drawing the line strictly between them and those of the Pennsylvania Road. Roxy ... will pick out one railroad man or another of the Long Island and spend a term of days with him. Then, not wishing to wear his welcome out, he will pass on to the next favorite.[12]

As Roxey got older, he expanded his riding companions from railroad employees to passengers aboard the trains. Roy Budd, a traveling salesman from Brooklyn, was one of Roxey's favorite traveling companions. Roxey would ride with Roy, dine with him at hotels, and once stayed with him for an entire week, sharing a room. Roy was with Roxey in April 1911 when he took his first train to Penn Station. Manhattan's Penn Station occupied two city blocks and was a formidable place for a wandering pup. One day Roxey boarded the wrong train at Penn Station and wound up in Philadelphia instead of his intended destination. It was a rare mistake for the experienced LIRR traveler. Otherwise, he never missed a connection and always landed in the right place.

Roxey met and made friends with many commuters over the years. One story reported that as the train arrived at the Broad Street station, the yellow dog dashed down the platform, did a few spins around, barked, and then sniffed out a New York train on his way back.[13] He arrived back in Queens at the Jamaica station in time to greet the Amagansett Express train from Montauk Point. Phil Norris, the engine driver, served up Roxey's weekly seafood dinner from Montauk. Then Roxey spent the night in Jamaica with the stationmaster.[14]

3. Roxey

Although this social dog might sometimes follow passengers home for a meal, he always returned to his railroad excursions the next day. Roxey knew New York. He made the acquaintance of the president of the Ladies' Kennel Association, Mrs. Alexander Butler Duncan, and many New York policemen.[15] Mrs. Duncan picked up Roxey near Central Park and carried him back to Long Island City, but she reported that Roxey turned back the next day and resumed his journey.[16]

Roxey was said to have spent Easter 1905 in Merrick. He returned wearing a blue ribbon on his collar with the report, "I spent Easter at Merrick and had a daisy time." Roxey fans speculated that he had visited Elsie Hess, a school teacher who lived near the Merrick station. Roxey would visit her, receive a drumstick at Christmas, and spend the night in a wicker basket she provided for the weary traveler.[17]

The LIRR and Penn Station

The LIRR was bound to attract a young vagabond dog in search of family, adventure, new sights, smells, and sounds. Railroads stimulated Americans' imaginations. The unconventional LIRR was unique in the era of colossal railroad conglomerates—a small, unorthodox railroad barely tolerated by those who depended on it. The little commuter railroad had a fascinating history and appeal as distinctive and unique as Roxey's.[18]

By 1850, an all-rail route between New York and Boston captured most of the travel business between the two cities. The LIRR eventually turned its attention away from Boston and focused on local town travel for the next few decades.[19] In 1880, Austin Corbin took control of the railroad, and his capital helped it develop and grow.

In the early 1900s, just one year before Roxey hopped on board, the LIRR had undergone significant changes. When Roxey appeared on the LIRR at the beginning of the 20th century, railroads had gained positions of power and influence. In 1900, the Pennsylvania Railroad purchased a controlling interest in the LIRR for $6 million. The Pennsylvania Railroad was a behemoth. It was the wealthiest and most powerful transportation company in North America and carried more passengers and freight than any other railroad. It was the leader in technology and operating practices in the railroad industry.

With the Pennsylvania Railroad acquiring control of the LIRR, the suburbs of Long Island bloomed. With the acquisition of its

Dogs of the Railways

competitors, the New York and Flushing and the South Ride Railway, the LIRR became the only railroad on Long Island and the first piggyback service. It modernized cars and purchased new ones, made plant improvements, improved service, and replaced electric engines with diesel engines on the nonelectric portion of the line. Thousands of commuters flocked from the city during peak rush hours. As a result of the new routes, middle- and upper-class families migrated to the suburbs. A boom of new residential homes in the 1920s followed in Jamaica, St. Albans, and Queens Village. The LIRR, strengthened by the financial resources of the Pennsylvania Railroad, was up to the challenge. By 1927, the LIRR had become the one first-class carrier to operate an all-passenger fleet.[20]

The Metropolitan Commuter Transportation Authority was created in 1965. In 1968, the Metropolitan Transportation Authority was formed; it now owns the LIRR.[21] Today, the LIRR is the busiest passenger railroad in the United States. On an average weekday, it carries over 350,000 passengers. It grew from 404 miles in 1929 to 701 miles by 2012 and now has 405 locomotives, 1,140 passenger cars, and 89 freight cars.[22]

The LIRR and Pennsylvania Railroad were incorporated to construct the extension of the New York tunnel from New Jersey through Manhattan to Long Island City in Queens and to build a new terminal. These two projects were landmark achievements of civil and electrical engineering and a visible testament to the triumph of American architecture. They also brought both Pennsylvania zone lines and those of its newly acquired LIRR subsidiary under the Hudson in the East River to a new Manhattan station and the new Hell Gate Bridge. This linked Pennsylvania to New England for freight passenger traffic.[23]

Penn Station played a starring role in the story of Roxey, New York, and LIRR. The station was a formidable building and monument to America's finest technology and construction at the time. It must have seemed like a universe of sounds, people, motion, smells, and clatter to even the most adventuresome of dogs, but Roxey added Penn Station to his itinerary. Penn Station would be a formidable transfer station for even the most experienced commuter, especially a vagabond raildog.

In 1900, when the Pennsylvania Railroad gained control of the LIRR, rail access to Manhattan was critical to its success. The original Penn Station project was completed in 1910. It was a mammoth undertaking, and the LIRR was included in the planning for the new station.[24]

3. Roxey

A small portion of Penn Station opened on September 8, 1910, in conjunction with the opening of the East River Tunnels. As a result, LIRR riders gained direct railroad service to Manhattan.[25] When Penn Station officially opened to the public in November 1910, between Saturday night and Sunday morning, more than 100,000 spectators and 25,000 passengers visited the station. By 1945, more than 100 million passengers would travel through Penn Station.[26]

The station was one of the most outstanding architectural achievements of its time. It covered nearly eight acres, extended two city blocks from Seventh Avenue to Eighth Avenue and from 31st to 33rd Streets, and housed one of the largest public spaces in the world..[27] The vision for the station was a monumental gateway to a great city inspired by Roman models of architecture. At its completion, it was admired for its grandeur and functionality for heavy commuter traffic. Along with Grand Central Station on 42nd Street, Penn Station provided a source of tremendous civic pride for New Yorkers.[28]

Penn Station represented a challenge for a traveling Roxey to find his way when he visited Manhattan. It was a cavernous building. As Roxey traveled through the great portal to Manhattan, Pennsylvania Station was like a small city that employed hundreds and hosted thousands daily. In 1939, the station had its biggest year until World War II, with nearly 220,000 passengers arriving or departing each day and nearly 100,000 or more passing through. More than 2,200 railroad employees worked in the station. A police force of 32 men was on duty to care for drunks, locate the parents of lost children, and protect the public from panhandlers. Pickpockets loved it. Thieves and con-men frequented the crowded station. Keeping order could be a daunting task for station police.[29] The grandeur of its public spaces and the excitement of arrivals and departures made Penn Station a favorite subject for artists. Writers found inspiration in the human drama that often plays out in a vast train station.

Penn Station was torn down in 1964. It was only 54 years old. An overburdened tax structure also contributed to the grand station's demise. It was torn down in part in the name of progress. Architects, historians, and railroad fans protested in vain. Norvel White, chairman of the Action Group for Better Architecture in New York, expressed New Yorkers' feelings: "They appreciated the old Penn Station. It was spacious, graceful, and elegant. It was said that the station made a ceremony of arrival and that you knew when you got off the train, you had arrived somewhere important."[30]

The grand building designed to last 800 years fought to survive its demolition. It took almost as long to demolish Penn Station as it had to build it.[31]

But even the demolition could not erase the grand terminal's legacy. A side effect of the tunneling project was to open the city up to the suburbs, and within ten years of opening, two-thirds of the daily passengers coming through Penn Station were commuters.[32] Penn Station offered the Pennsylvania Railroad a comparative advantage over its competitors, offering direct service from Manhattan to the west and south. Because of its involvement in the Penn Station project, LIRR pioneered firsts such as mainline electrification with 600 volts in 1905 and the first all-steel passenger car fleet in 1927. Still, the LIRR eventually struggled to be profitable as a commuter enterprise.

One of the Boys

The Long Island Railroad played a vital part in life on Long Island. In the 1920s, the party spirit of the era often prevailed—just the kind of place to attract a sporty young pup. The Sunrise Trail Band was a musical treat featured on and around the island.[33] They rode special trains in Greenport and performed on the way to New London. Roxey must have enjoyed the traveling band as they rode through. The LIRR, in conjunction with the Pennsylvania Railroad, sponsored an athletic program. It wasn't a small program—it required $2 million of the Pennsylvania Railroad budget. In 1920, the LIRR began sponsoring intramural sports. From 1923 to 1931, over 700 of the railroad's 13,000 employees participated.

Roxey was officially one of the boys in the railroad community and had a credential to prove it. The raildog was a fully elected lifetime member of the YMCA without dues. Roxey was a fan of the five-story Long Island branch of the YMCA at 45 Borden Avenue. It sat across from the rail yard, and the canine commuter enjoyed his evenings there between 1901 and 1913. The YMCA was founded in 1844 and began its work among railroad men in Cleveland, Ohio. A railroad employee who had reformed from drinking invited a minister to preach to railroad men in the station's waiting room. Crowds of people came, and the gathering evolved into a revival, which gave birth to the first branch of the YMCA composed of railroad men. The YMCA provided affordable meals, overnight accommodations, and programs for the railroad men.

3. Roxey

It featured a library, cafeteria, gymnasium, dormitories for the men, and an excellent place for a respite for a raildog to enjoy a brief break from his travels.

The railroad staff considered Roxey part of the family and felt the pup was a good luck ambassador. Like most railroads, the LIRR was filled with its perils. In December 1880, snowdrifts led to one of the most fantastic train wrecks, often called "the Great Snow Blockade." On August 26, 1893, two trains collided in Maspeth, Queens, killing 16 people and injuring more than 40. In April 1914, it was a sunny Easter morning, but heavy wet snow clogged the railroad, and several trains derailed.[34] In July 1915, Engine 16 broke the axle of her main driver near Blue Point on the Montauk division. Residents of Suffolk hopped on their bicycles and packed lunches to see the big engine fallen in shame. Camelback Steam Engine No. 16 accommodated Suffolk County residents' burgeoning interest in train catastrophes. On September 28, 1922, Engine Number 91 split at Centre Moriches. One passenger refused to leave the derailed coach until train crew members convinced him he could not move for eight hours. He was helped to board another train.[35]

The precarious travel on the Long Island rails challenged a vagabond dog with various perils. Still, Roxey survived. One day he got off the train at Freeport, Long Island, and did not see an express train coming in the opposite direction. Passengers waiting on the platform shrieked as they saw the engine, but Roxey did not see it coming. Miraculously one by one, the train cars rolled over the small canine. As the last one passed over Roxey, the observers were astonished when the sturdy dog stood on his legs, turned around a few times, and then inspected himself to convince himself he was in one piece. He proceeded to finish his encounter with a dog fight.[36] In June 1902, an automobile driven by a chauffeur ran over Roxey. In 1905, Roxey suffered a broken leg from a stone thrown at him. He wore a splint for several weeks.

Fortunately, as a treasured companion of the LIRR, Roxey received excellent veterinary care. Commuters even set up a personal bank account for him at the Corn Exchange Bank in Long Island City for medical needs. When Roxey was hit by an automobile in Hempstead, Mr. Peters, president of the railroad, placed him under the care of a veterinarian until the injured dog recovered.[37] Roxey also encountered the third rail at Jamaica and received a severe electric shock but recovered; some claimed the aging dog never regained his robust health.[38] Roxey continued to travel the baggage car run for almost 15 years until old age banished him to a veterinary hospital in Jamaica.

A Dog Among Dogs

Eventually, old age and his heavy travel caught up with Roxey. In his old age, he still traveled but had difficulty mounting and descending train car steps. His breathing sounded labored. His admiring fans noticed their friend's decline. An anonymous friend of Roxey penned a note on Roxey's behalf, printed it on cards, and distributed it to the railroad men. While Roxey wasn't the author, it seemed to express the sentiment he might express if he could talk.

> To the officers and employees of the LIRR:
>
> Feeling that I am at the end of life's journey, I appeal to you to bury me near where the passing of trains will bring me in death as in life, near "the boys"—where they can see the grave of the little dog that loved them so well.
> ROXEY[39]

On June 11, 1914, Roxey died at the home of Dr. W.L. Johnson in Jamaica. Newspapers reported the demise of Long Island's favorite dog. The *South Side Signal* eulogized him, claiming, "He had a nose for news and listened closely."[40] Newspapers across New York reported Roxey's death as an admiring public mourned his passing. On June 18, 1914, the *Sun* newspaper reported the death of Roxey and proposed what endeared the loyal dog to the citizenry of Long Island.[41]

> Roxey counted many as his friends and had many mourners. He was considered a mild-mannered, friendly dog and good to have as a friend. Roxey's greatest asset was that he made no social or moral distinctions in who he chose as a friend and that humans would be better if they shared some of Roxey's traits. He was "a dog among dogs."[42]
>
> So as Cesar was a king's dog, so Roxey was the LIRR dog.[43]

The *Nassau Daily Review–Star* declared that the little dog "had more publicity than any other dog known."[44]

His railroad family buried Roxey near the right of way at Merrick station on railroad property adjoining the train station. Pallbearers included the foreman of the LIRR electric department and the foreman of the high tension department. In 1952, a new Merrick parking field was constructed at the site, but the grave of the LIRR mascot was left undisturbed. Twenty years later, in June 1934, a monument was placed

3. Roxey

Pennsylvania Railroad Station exterior, View from Gimbels, 1911, New York, New York (Library of Congress, Photographs Division).

on Roxey's grave. At the ceremony, the Rev. John Gerstenberg of the Church of the Redeemer read a "Prayer for a Dog" and memorialized Roxey as "a good dog who will never be forgotten."

Roxey, the commuter canine of the LIRR, was buried in granite in the presence of two foremen of the electrical department and several commuters who let several trains go by while they paid a last tribute to the dog of the LIRR.

Roxey's gravesite was well tended at first but fell into disrepair later.[45] His grave no longer sits in sight of the railroad since the old two-lane road past it that had the trains at grade level has been replaced by the new elevated railroad and widened highway. A tiny gravesite sits east of Merrick Avenue along Sunrise Highway, against the guard rail.[46] On the north side of Sunrise Highway, west of the intersection with Merrick Avenue, visitors can pull into the parking lot for the Merrick station. But Roxey's grave is not forgotten. People still come by to leave flowers and clean out the water bowl built in the gravesite base in honor of Roxey's memory.

Roxey's legacy continues in another way. In May 2000, Heather Hill Worthington wrote the book *Miles of Smiles: The Story of Roxey, the Long Island Rail Road Dog.*[47] A special ceremony was held to

Dogs of the Railways

commemorate and honor Roxey's life and the book's publication. At the event, LIRR President Helena Williams remarked, "The humanity and dedication shown to Roxey are traits that continue to shine brightly today among our employees and customers. We hope Roxey's story will inspire excitement about rail travel among a whole new generation of LIRR railroad customers."[48]

4

Sheba's Bob

Dog Detective of the Long Island Railroad, 1906–1916

The station attendant at the Long Island Railroad (LIRR) freight house at Valley Stream discovered the break-in at 7:30 AM. He hurried to alert gateman Robert Earle that thieves had stolen several grocery items and other goods. Marks on the window frame indicated it had been forced open.

Earle asked Smith, "Who do you suppose done it?"

Smith said, "Sheba's Bob will find out. I'll telephone for him right away."

Earle agreed. "Yes, if anyone can find the burglars, Sheba's Bob can."[1]

Sheba's Bob, canine railroad detective, was about to sniff out another crime. By 9:30 AM, Sheba's Bob and his partner dog, Jim, arrived at the crime scene ready and eager to track down the perpetrator. Sheba's Bob was big enough to impress a burglar up to no good. When he stood on his hind legs, the bloodhound could look a grown man directly in the eye. Bob had a long, wrinkled face with loose skin; huge, drooping ears that touched the floor; and deep-set eyes. He strode into an assignment with an expression of solemn dignity like a five-star general ready to deploy the troops. Bob's powerful legs could push him to follow a scent over miles of punishing terrain. Bloodhounds can weigh up to 110 pounds. He may have been huge, but Sheba's Bob moved like a locomotive.

The search for the perpetrator of the freight house break-in continued as Station Agent Smith recalled that he had seen a man around the freight house at 2 AM, 7½ hours before. The two canine detectives picked up the burglar's scent, and their bloodhound noses went to work and began their pursuit. The dogs' handler, Lieutenant Miller, struggled to hold back the powerful dogs and hurried to keep up with their pace. Sheba's Bob got the scent, took one leap off the platform as straight as an *arrow, and soared through the air in pursuit as he followed his nose to trail the burglar to the railroad track. The lumbering canine on the run dragged Miller down the railroad track, scrambled up an embankment, and pulled him directly to the back of the water station. The team of dogs moved back to the tracks and started to run with their noses skimming the ground. They dragged Miller further down the tracks and jumped over a barbed wire. The dogs then headed into the woods, still dragging their handler. The dogs discovered Frederick Reising skimming a muskrat in a tool shed in the back. Bob was the first to jump on Reising.*

"Take him away!" Reising yelled.[2]

Next, Bob darted for the barn and ran up the stairs on the side of the building. He ran through the kitchen and down the hall and started to howl at a trunk in the bedroom. Inside the trunk were goods stolen from the freight house. Following the arrest of Frederick Reising, police found other items in the barn where he was hiding, including about 40 bicycles (one of them rigged as a getaway bike), silver, and glassware. In a private residence nearby, detectives also found several gold and silver watches, other articles of jewelry, and dynamite. The Washington Post *in reporting the caper declared Sheba's Bob "a real Sherlock Holmes."*[3] *The dog detectives of the LIRR had solved another case.*

* * *

A Crime Wave Plagues the LIRR

From 1909 to 1916, Sheba's Bob was the LIRR's secret weapon against crime. He was a clever bloodhound with a set of colossal ears and a nose that wouldn't quit. Sheba's Bob and three of his dog detective colleagues partnered with the LIRR police to solve crimes during a crime wave that threatened the LIRR. In two years on the job, they captured 100 or more thieves, disclosed the location of a murderer, and recovered at least 15 lost children who returned home to their parents.

It wasn't just train wrecks and accidents that plagued the LIRR. The LIRR had a crime problem.[4] Railroad communities lured scoundrels, robbers, and thieves.[5] A typical railroad town featured a train station, post office, general store, and a few houses, and some towns had a hotel. All were targets for criminals.

By 1860, railroads' westward extension in the United States had established over 20,000 miles of railroad with settlers, boomtowns, and

4. Sheba's Bob

adventure seekers, and crime followed.[6] Through the early 1900s, train station burglaries, gunfights, and murders plagued the railroads. Rail passengers and workers encountered dangers from criminals. Thieves overpowered rail crews, dynamited railcars and railroad structures and stole property and freight. In addition, criminals would create opportunities to rob rail commuters and passengers by attempting to cause a train wreck by laying rail or boulders across the tracks. As a result, railroad police and passengers were wounded or killed. Stopping a train for nefarious purposes was as easy as simply waving a red lantern in front of the train and flagging it to a stop.[7]

Train station and post office burglaries were typical, and gunfights and murders haunted the peaceful residents living around the railroad. In 1908, many post office burglaries occurred in villages along the tracks from Queens to Nassau County. Over three years, a band of dangerous burglars who dynamited station safes and even private residences terrorized Long Island.[8] Residents of Mineola Village became so accustomed to the sounds of nitroglycerin blowing the post office safe open that they ignored it with "it's only the post office being blown."[9] The Mineola post office became known as "America's safe-blowing belt."

Gangs of robbers remained a problem for railroads until the end of the century and beyond. Robberies had an impact on railroad companies. With no organized law enforcement, vigilante groups were organized to maintain law and order. These disorganized groups failed to prevent the crimes, leaving the railroad communities vulnerable to criminal activity. Thefts of luggage, livestock, and freight continued on the railroads.

What made the railroad and a railroad community such a target, and why did railroad crimes proliferate? In 2017, Rudell and Decker studied the history of railroad robberies between 1866 and 1930 to explain the origins of growth and how to eradicate similar crimes. They attributed the spread of train robberies in this period to several factors: the large population of unemployed civil war veterans; antipathy, anger, and hostility toward the railroad companies in the Midwestern and Western states; the attractiveness of trains as targets; the low population density in the West; the lack of coordinated law enforcement; newspaper glamorization of these offenses and the offenders; and the minimal training required to become a train robber.[10]

The railroads needed their own police departments, and they knew

Dogs of the Railways

it. It was no job for the fainthearted. Many railroad agents died protecting railroad employees, passengers, and goods. The railroads began to hire security guards to guard freight in the rail yards. With no training, the guards were handed a gun, badge, and a club and told to go out and protect the railroad property and employees.

Two titles evolved for the railroad police. Most departments in the East used the title "detective" for railroad police, while "special agent" was the title for railroad police in the West. Eastern railroads used uniformed officers to prevent crime and disorder. Western railroads worked with sheriffs and U.S. marshals. They wore plain clothes and conducted investigative work. These titles are still used today in modern railroad policing. In 1865, the Pennsylvania Legislature enacted the Railroad Police Act of 1865. This act authorized the governor of the state to grant police power to any individual for whom the employing railroad petitioned. In addition, it gave railroad police officers statewide authority.[11]

Railroad crew members were sometimes called upon to protect their trains. These trainmen, who usually had no authority, fought tramps and vagrants who rode their trains and stole from the freight cars and passengers. Some trainmen were quite creative and occasionally conducted their own investigations; some used surveillance to detect the criminal. For example, in 1875, a brakemen solved a crime in which hogs were being stolen from the Chicago and North Western Railroad as they were shipped to stockyards in Chicago from Clinton, Iowa. A brakemen attempted to solve the hog thefts and hid in a small cage built for the hogs. When the train stopped for water and coal, the brakeman crouched in the cage. A group of thieves then attempted to drive the hogs from the pen. To the criminals' shock, the clever brakeman hopped out the cage, surprised the felons and the thieves were apprehended.

Secret Service agents attached to the post office and local authorities, along with the LIRR, all worked to track down the perpetrators. But unfortunately, their efforts did little to prevent crimes. The railroad police needed help. They hired contractors to investigate losses climbing into the millions of dollars. The LIRR police officers rode motorcycles, and some used automobiles to chase bicycles to pursue robbers, but the crimes continued.[12] In 1908, post offices and private residence robberies were reported in villages along the tracks.

In 1923, the Pennsylvania Railroad Police Act created the railroad police as a police organization with the powers of arrest to protect the

4. Sheba's Bob

railroads against criminals. Because there were still few railroad police and many routes the railroads traveled had no law enforcement, this act gave the train's conductor temporary police powers to protect passengers, employees, and railroad freight. A railroad police officer could be maimed or killed.

Travel on the LIRR had increased congestion on the Jamaica platforms so much that it had become necessary to have a uniformed platform squad. So in the spring of 1920, the superintendent of police of the LIRR set into motion a uniformed team of LIRR policemen who became the LIRR Platform Squad. This initiative resulted in increased order, prevention of congestion, and more rapid and harmonious handling of the thousands of commuters.[13]

When other policing efforts proved futile, the railroad turned to dogs for help. Bloodhounds were about to come to the rescue of the LIRR. Crime-fighting dogs were not a new idea. Dogs liked trains and could travel well on moving cars if necessary. The skill set of certain breeds made them ideal candidates for police recruits. Many police dogs were bloodhounds, and other hound-like dogs whose expert tracking talent could sniff out nefarious activities. Dogs have been involved in police and detective work for hundreds of years. English and French police forces used dogs regularly in the 1880s and 1890s. Later, Belgium and Germany implemented the first formalized and dedicated training programs for police dogs. Long Island Railroad Superintendent Robert E. Kirkham had learned about these results and purchased two English bloodhounds named Bob and Nellie, who produced seven pups, one of whom died. Kirkham had the remaining six trained for detective duty.

The "Greatest of Dog Detectives"

> "We had tried policemen on bicycles, motorcycles, and even automobiles to run down plunderers, but had poor results until we got the dogs."—Long Island Railroad Police Superintendent Robert E. Kirkham[14]

When Superintendent Robert E. Kirkham of the LIRR police brought bloodhound recruits on the team, he had recruited a set of noses that were the rock stars of tracking bad guys. The American Kennel Club says the world-famous sleuth hound "does one thing better than any creature on earth: find people who are lost or hiding. An

Dogs of the Railways

off-duty bloodhound is among the canine kingdom's most docile citizens, but he's relentless and stubborn on scent."[15]

Sheba's Bob and his team of floppy ears and noses to the ground were just the investigators for the job. Bob was ready and physically up for the challenge of keeping the railroad community safe and bringing criminals to justice. The work of the bloodhound detectives resulted in a drop in crime on the railroad, especially the dynamiting of station safes and thefts.

Duty often summoned a raildog detective. In February 1911, several attempts were made to wreck the Wading River Express Train, also known as the "Gaynor Special." New York's "Tammany Hall" Mayor William Jay Gaynor—the only mayor to be hit by a bullet during an assassination attempt—always used this train to travel to his country home in St. James on Saturdays. The bloodhounds tracked the criminal's trail and led to the arrest of a man in Long Island City. Several case occurred when residents went missing. The entire community might search day and night with no result. Finally, a call would go into the Long Island Police headquarters, and the bloodhounds were deployed. Sometimes in just hours after starting their search, the dogs could locate the missing person.[16]

As crime continued, the dog detectives were busy. The contents of a ticket box on the East End were stolen, and the burglar took off with a 12-hour start on the detective dogs. Sheba's Bob and his pals trailed him, and he was captured. Wires were being cut on the Manhattan Beach Division. It put the signals out of order and impacted the movement of the trains. The bloodhounds picked up the scent from the steel rails and followed them to an East New York liquor store and from there to the thief's house. Thieves robbed the Catholic Church at Westbury, and the dogs tracked the burglars; the vessels stolen from the church were recovered.

Property owners along the railroad line benefited from the protection of the bloodhound raildogs as they trailed and captured nefarious sorts. Sheba's Bob was declared the "greatest of dog detectives" by New York newspapers.[17]

The dogs honed their skills. An expert trainer trained Sheba's Bob and the dogs to practice their tracking skills and make sure the dogs would be in top form at the shortest notice. The dogs became feared and hated by the criminals, and several unsuccessful attempts were made to poison them. The dogs were then never let loose and were trained never to accept food from anyone other than their handlers.[18]

4. Sheba's Bob

A celebrated case occurred when a child went missing and neighbors formed a search party, but after 27 hours, the LIRR police were finally asked to bring their bloodhounds to the beach. The dogs sniffed the girl's shoes and stockings, and four hours later, they tracked the child to a spot five miles away. The little girl was fast asleep on the grass, only four feet from the edge of a deep creek. Said Kirkham: "One man and a well-chilled bloodhound are worth more than six ordinary patrolmen in in-country work."[19]

Sheba's Bob's Legacy: Today's Special Agent

As change came to the railroads, it also came to railroad policing. The benefits of the dog detectives and so-called "K9 units" in the spirit of Sheba's Bob rose to the challenge with a new skill set, new challenges, and new risks. A technological and specialized system of policing evolved to meet the new challenges. In the early and mid–1940s, thousands of railroad police officers worked in the United States and Canada.[20] By the mid–1940s, rail had become the primary mode of transportation across the United States, and the railroad police officer's scope of responsibility expanded. An officer was responsible for the safety of cargo and passengers, both on and off the train. In addition, railroad police officers were often staged at railroad depots to watch for criminals.

As rail travel decreased, the rail police force downsized. Smaller, more powerful locomotives make fewer stops and travel at higher speeds. As trains stop less frequently and for a shorter amount of time, the opportunity to burglarize railcars diminished. But new threats of terrorism took the place of train robberies, creating new demands for a railroad policing presence. High-value freight may be enclosed in specially designed railcars. Rail police use modern technology to better secure and protect cargo transit.

Today, although usually paid by the railroad companies themselves, railroad police officers have the authority to conduct investigations and make arrests for crimes committed against the railroad. Some agencies, such as Amtrak police, also attend the Federal Law Enforcement Training Academy as part of their training. Today's railroad police work depots and railroad property either by foot or car and investigate cargo theft, vandalism, theft of equipment, arson, train/vehicle collisions, and even assault and murders on railroad property. During patrols, officers

Dogs of the Railways

are alert for persons trespassing on railroad property. Although some trespassers may be looking for a chance to commit a crime, often these trespassers are pedestrians taking shortcuts along the tracks or across the rail yard, not realizing how dangerous the railroad tracks and yards can be.

As modern police forces developed, so did the role of the contemporary police dog. Today, dogs work alongside the police as part of the law enforcement workforce; they even take oaths and have badges. Today's police dogs are trained in the detection of explosives and of illegal substances. At retirement, these dogs often make their permanent home with their handlers. (See Chapter 9 for a discussion of today's canine Guardian of the Railways.)

Today the Metropolitan Transportation Authority (MTA) Police Department patrols the trains, stations, tracks, and yards of the LIRR, Metro-North Railroad, and Staten Island Railway. The MTA Police Department's Canine Unit was established in 2002 to protect rail customers from terrorism and other criminal acts. The dogs also help reduce railroad service disruptions by expediting inspections of unattended packages.[21] The raildogs support the MTA's security strategy in ways other tools could never do; MTA Police Department Lieutenant John Kerwick is a believer: "Canines can do in minutes what can take hours for humans to do when searching for explosives or other evidence in crimes…. 'Our Canine Unit team is incredibly dedicated,' said MTAPD Lt. John Kerwick."[22]

The role of the railroad dog detective has evolved side by side with that of the human officer, as will be seen in Chapter 9 on raildog K9 patrols. Sheba's Bob, the "greatest dog detective," and the detective dogs of the LIRR pioneered the way for the modern canine guardians of the railways. Perhaps in spirit they still patrol the railroad with their modern canine counterparts, noses to the ground, strolling the railroad grounds as new recruits learn the art of being a raildog scent hound.

5

Annie

The Colorado Southern Railway Ambassador of Kindness, 1934–1948

Four burly railroad men struggled to lift the pregnant dog onto the train. She wiggled and grunted, but these railroad men were strong enough to load the reluctant canine mother. They packed her tenderly into the caboose.

The crew had just returned from their daily route on the Colorado Southern through Greeley, Windsor, Timnath, and Fort Collins. The railroad men found the dog living at the back of the Timnath Blacksmith Shop, a noisy, filthy place filled with the smell of black smoke. A horse had once kicked the dog. The blacksmith told the train crew members that he was only too glad to be rid of the expectant mother. The blacksmith might not want her, but the men of the Colorado Southern did. They took pity on the small mother-to-be. They tucked her into the red caboose, and she traveled home with them back to the Fort Collins depot. On the way, the railmen considered that their boss might not want to have a dog hanging around. Still, they put aside their misgivings and took her to the basement of the depot. The dog was shivering, so they put an old coat around her and placed her in a cardboard box near the furnace. They gave her lunch, water, and a family.

The Colorado and Southern Railroad men decided to call the dog Annie, the railroad dog. Annie went on to live as a permanent resident of the depot and became a Fort Collins celebrity. The crew's worries about the boss not allowing dogs at the depot turned out to be unfounded; Annie became the only exception to the no-dogs-allowed policy.[1] Instead of the sounds of the blacksmith shop, Annie listened to the sounds of train whistles and footsteps and the telegraph clicking. When her time arrived,

Dogs of the Railways

Annie presented her rescuers with three black and white puppies. When they were weaned, the plump and bouncy puppies were given to three children who loved them. Annie was spayed to prevent unwanted future litters.

Annie remained as part of the Colorado Southern railroad family and the Fort Collins community. Annie's life as a raildog was a testament to the enduring power of kindness even in the most challenging times. Through the kindness of the railroad family, she went on to thrive for 14 years. During drought, war, and the Great Depression, she served as a source of comfort and love to the residents of Fort Collins.[2]

* * *

Times were tough in Fort Collins in 1935, and food was sometimes hard to come by. The Great Depression hit Fort Collins hard and was made worse by a farming downturn. As a result, many Fort Collins residents were hungry and struggled to feed their families. The county even rented a 7-acre garden in 1935 so county dependents could raise food for themselves. Yet, in this time of hardship, the men of the Colorado Southern had felt compassion for a pregnant dog and carried her to the warm and welcoming Fort Collins depot. On that one day in 1935, at least one mother-to-be did not go hungry.

Fort Collins sits along the front range of the Rocky Mountains on the Cache la Poudre River in Larimer County, Colorado. It was initially founded as a U.S. Army post in 1864. In 1872, a population explosion brought settlers and an agricultural economy, followed by commercial and residential development and sheep slaughtering industries. But at the end of World War I, prices fell for agricultural goods, and the Fort Collins farming economy declined.

By the time the Great Depression hit Fort Collins, tough times had already arrived. During the first half of the decade, plains farmers lost crops due to drought and a grasshopper plague. In 1934, a water shortage in Fort Collins reached such critical levels city residents were banned from using water from the waterworks system for lawns and gardens. In addition, the Cache la Poudre River was reportedly at its lowest since the valley's settlement.[3]

Work was hard to find, and unemployment soared. By March 1935, about 11,500 persons, nearly 35 percent of the county's population, received federal or county relief.[4] The relief program attempted to help farmers and those without jobs. Farmers could access seed and

5. Annie

feed loans and pay when their crops were sold. Hundreds of men went to work on county improvement work programs of the Civil Works Administration.[5] Through prosperous times and hardship in Fort Collins, one thing was constant. Trains rolled through town and were critical to Fort Collins.

The railroad was at the heart of Annie's story. Railroads created new possibilities for Annie and the people of her adopted town. Fort Collins lacked the shipping capabilities that moving supplies and equipment required. The wagon roads from Fort Collins to Denver and Cheyenne were passable only in good weather. Railroads brought the means to bring manufacturers' building materials from the East. The Colorado Central reached Fort Collins in 1877; the Greeley, Salt Lake, and Pacific followed in 1882. Ansel Watrous wrote in his book, *The History of Larimer County*, "that the railroad changed the history of Fort Collins and Larimer County. It allowed the farmer and stockman to ship their surplus products and fat cattle to broader and better markets."[6]

The Colorado Southern was formed as a consolidation of bankrupt railroads in 1898 when the Colorado Southern acquired the Colorado Central Railroad and then the Greeley, Salt Lake, and Pacific (GSL&P) in 1882. The Union Pacific subsidiaries were later consolidated into the Colorado & Southern (C&S) Railway in 1898. The Colorado and Southern Railroad operated in Wyoming, Colorado, and New Mexico. In Texas, the Colorado and Southern controlled a rail system that included ten railroads, of which eight were owned by the end of 1910.[7] In December 1908, the Chicago, Burlington and Quincy Railroad Company purchased the Colorado and Southern although the Colorado and Southern continued to operate as a separate company. On March 2, 1970, the Burlington was one of the railroads merged to form the Burlington Northern Railroad, and the Colorado and Southern was subsequently merged on December 31, 1981.[8]

During Annie's time on the rails, the C&S was still a busy depot, although later, the period was felt to be the railroad era's "sunset years."[9] Annie's home, the Fort Collins depot, was completed in 1911 and served the area livestock industry and sugar beet and lumber enterprises. The freight depot was a 50-foot long wooden deck that could accommodate up to 12 railroad cars at one time. Although the railroad industry never achieved its earlier glory, the C&S depot made history as the longest continuously used rail facility in the region.[10]

Raildog for Fort Collins: A Friendly Greeter in Good Times and Bad

Annie raised spirits for Fort Collins in tough times. She cheered the railroad family through the Great Depression, a drought, and World War II and became a devoted community dog to the Fort Collins community. In the 1940s, Fort Collins was a small town, and Annie's rounds could cover both the rails and the town. She would ride the train to Denver and back.

A friendly and pleasant pup, she was treated to scraps and food as she visited with the train- and townspeople. The butcher saved scraps for Annie. She shuffled between the homes of Fort Collins, where town people welcomed her. People in the Northern Hotel liked to pet her. Sometimes fans came out of the soda fountain and gave Annie a dip of ice cream. Some observers noted that as Annie grew older, she grew plump from treats from her admirers. Everyone knew Annie and looked out for her. She became a celebrity.

Annie took up a steady job as the greeter at the passenger depot and the freight depot. One Fort Collins story claims that Annie licked the tears from the faces of weeping soldiers returning from World War II and that some passengers who got off the train greeted Annie before they greeted their own families.[11]

Brakeman Christopher Demuth was one of the men who brought the stray dog to Fort Collins in her time of need. When Chris retired, so did Annie from her greeter job, and in their mutual retirement, he and Annie took walks and continued greeting the town.

When Annie died in her bed in 1948 at age 14, Demuth and the railroad crew buried her in the graveyard near the depot she had loved and put up a headstone inscribed, "From the C&S Men to Annie, Our Dog, 1934–1948." Lifelong Fort Collins resident Charles Hagenmeister said, "People loved that dog. They would always feed her. People that rode that train still remembers her. She was just like a fire station's dog."[12] Arlene Ahlbrandt, writing in *Annie, The Railroad Dog: A True Story*, reported that a mystery person placed colorful artificial flowers on Annie's grave at different times of the year for many years.[13]

Annie's memory endures. When the Fort Collins depot was renovated decades later, the town sprang into action to prevent Annie's grave from being moved or eliminated. In 1995, Fort Collins purchased the depot and Annie's grave and designated both as local landmarks. The State Historical Fund awarded a grant to Fort Collins in 1996, which

5. Annie

allowed the depot to be restored and Annie's gravesite to be fenced and repainted. In August 2001, the C&S freight depot reopened as the Fort Collins transit center and functions as a vital component of the city's revitalization.[14] Loretta Burdette, daughter of Demuth, the brakeman on the No. 60, was asked how the original rescuers of Annie might feel about her grave being designated with honor. She replied, "That would make all those men feel so wonderful." She said of her father and the four other crewmen who rescued Annie, "They were all instrumental in bringing the dog over and finding a home for the puppies."[15]

Annie's Legacy: A Testament to Kindness

Annie's story lives on through an educational video on Facebook through the Fort Collins Museum online archive collection. Children can watch a video and do activities to learn about Annie and celebrate her and the other animals in their lives.[16] Young visitors to Annie's site on Daily Discovery, at the Fort Collins Museum of Discovery website, are encouraged to keep Annie's spirit alive by being kind to animals in their life. Annie's message perfectly fits the library as she welcomes visitors with a raised paw. Loretta Demuth Burdette said in an interview, "Annie was a sweetheart and seemed to understand her special status; she waited against the wall until someone beckoned her to be petted."[17]

Annie has become an ambassador for the humane treatment of animals and kindness and mercy to animals. It's an important mission for Annie. When children are educated to show kindness to animals, they become more kind and compassionate in their interactions with animals and one another. Stories that cultivate kindness to animals can be the starting point of education that promotes more humane citizens. Humane education encourages many character values, including compassion, respect, empathy, and inclusion.[18] A story like Annie's can forge a connection between people and convey shared values that unite a community as they become engaged in understanding an abstract concept such as kindness, compassion, empathy, or resilience in the face of adversity.

When educators and parents try to explain abstract concepts like kindness or generosity to children, it can be challenging. Abstract concepts can be hard to explain and often need concrete examples. But stories, especially about animals, make abstract ideas clearer. Annie's story describes kind acts and compassionate behavior and emphasizes

Dogs of the Railways

the interconnectedness of all of us who cohabit this world. A tale of a dog that was helped by kind humans and returned the love to an entire town can demonstrate what we believe about how we should treat each other. Dog stories open doors to understanding ideas and lessons that are sometimes difficult to access in other ways. A story about Annie and kindness provides children and adults a teachable moment about respect and empathy for all living creatures.

Annie's story works to show the principles of humane education for another reason. In Annie's story, we see that Annie is a dog, not a tiny human. She doesn't wear a costume, is not an object, and doesn't pretend to talk. Instead, we accept her for who she is, a wonderful dog who needed help, protection, and kindness from humans, and with that kindness, she flourished. Annie's story encourages understanding and helps children learn to be responsible humans in their relationships with other creatures who share our earth and appreciate their unique natures.

When sculptor Dawn Weimar heard Annie's story, she created a sculpture of the town's favorite dog. She sculpted the likeness from one photo she found of Annie with Demuth's daughter, Loretta Burdette. Weimar made 35 castings of Annie. One stands in front of the Fort Collins Regional Public Library, where Annie raises a paw to welcome visitors. The library organized an annual "Annie Walk and Pet Fest," where participants walked from the library to Annie's grave at the depot to celebrate the unveiling. The "Annie Walk" continued for 13 years until it ended in 2011.[19]

In 2014, in honor of Fort Collins' sesquicentennial, the *Coloradoan*, a daily newspaper of Fort Collins, named ten events that helped shape Fort Collins into the community it is today. The founding of the city, development of industry, the railroads, war, and other milestone events were named notable events but listed as number six was the arrival of a pregnant, mixed-breed dog named Annie in 1943. Said the *Coloradoan* in naming Annie, "The dog cheered workers during the dark days of World War II and became a well-known face for Fort Collins and the role of railroads in Fort Collins' commerce. At her death in 1948, C&S workers placed a gravestone in her honor. A statue of Annie rests at the Fort Collins downtown public library at 201 Peterson St., where the annual Annie Walk, a 5K, starts every year."[20]

The Burlington Northern Santa Fe rail line still travels through Fort Collins regularly. The trains that run down Mason Street are reminders of the long history between the community, the railroad, and

5. Annie

Annie the railroad dog with Christopher Demuth (1874–1952) in Fort Collins, Colorado (courtesy of Fort Collins History Connection, photo ID H10159).

a dog. The memory of Annie lingers at the depot in testament to the dog who knew the kindness of humans and went on to repay that kindness in Fort Collins' darkest hours. Even after she died in 1948, Annie left a legacy of the enduring power of kindness. More than 60 years later, her simple grave in Fort Collins is a testament to the railroad men's compassion for a little dog in her time of need and how she returned their love with a loyalty that still inspires new generations. Annie, the homeless mother dog, lives on today as a storyteller about the power of kindness.

6

Shep

*Faithfulness on the Great
Northern Railroad,
1931–1942*

The sheepdog whined and paced as two men loaded a wooden coffin onto a buckboard. No one noticed the dog. The men prepared to accompany a sheepherder's body to the Fort Benton, Montana, railroad station to begin a final train journey back east for burial. As the buckboard departed for the station, the dog leaped in and began to watch over the wooden coffin. The driver and undertaker ushered the dog out of the wagon. "No, not this trip, boy."

The canine ran behind the wagon the entire nine miles to the Fort Benton station. The dog paced back and forth at the station as the men loaded the coffin on the baggage car. As the men packed the dead sheepherder's paltry belongings into a sack to accompany his body to his final resting place, one of the men remarked, "Not much to remember for decades of a man's life."

The men loading the body are wrong.

The sheepherder and his dog will leave a legacy that becomes one of Montana's and America's greatest dog stories. It is the beginning of a 5½-year vigil that would be broken only by the sheepdog's death. This unbroken bond between a sheepherder and his dog will inspire a nation.

* * *

Once the coffin was loaded, the baggage door slammed shut, and the locomotive whistle blasted notice of departure. With a hiss of steam, it chugged further and further into the distance. As the Great Northern train lumbered slowly toward the river, the lone sheepdog, tail down, trotted down the tracks behind the train and then broke into a run as the train picked up speed.

6. Shep

The canine stopped for a brief moment, panting harder now, and watched the train go out of sight. The sheepdog got up and pressed on, following slower and slower. His feet bled on the rocky track bed, but the dog continued to follow the train into the night. With his last shred of energy, the sheepdog wandered step by step down to the river, drank, and slept.

The sheepdog greeted every incoming train as the days and weeks went by. He appeared at the station just in time to welcome new arrivals. The dog hid in the sagebrush on the hill until he heard the train's distant whistle. He knew directions. If a train approached from the west, he remained where he was. But when a train arrived from the east, he worked his way down the tracks and waited there. When the train was close enough, he leaped onto the platform, where he would greet passengers. He wagged his tail as the passengers stepped from the train. Would his sheepherder be the next face he would see?

For more than five years, the sheepdog met all four scheduled passenger trains and became a fixture on the Great Northern train station platform. Through the heat of Montana summers and the bitter cold of Montana winters, the dog inspected each arriving passenger looking for the return of his beloved guardian. When the dog had checked passengers from each train, he tucked his tail between his legs, jumped down from the platform, and loped back up the hill.

The men at the station sometimes left a sandwich or a piece of meat for the stray dog. Conductor Ed Shields and Section Foreman Pat McSweeney offered food and tried to convince him to enjoy a comfortable, warm bed beside a stove at the station, but the dog preferred his independence. He avoided hugging and petting, though he would wag his tail at the gift of a sandwich or other food. Sometimes the canine would get just close enough to older men to get a good sniff just to make sure a human wasn't his sheepherder handler.

The train crew members of the Great Northern grew fond of the stray canine and named him *Shep*, a name commonly used for sheepdogs. Steve McSweeney, son of Section Foreman McSweeney, and his mother Kitty began walking to the depot and offering table scraps to Shep. The McSweeneys started a campaign to win Shep's trust. Eventually, Shep let them pet him, but he could not be coaxed away from the depot to sleep. He preferred a nook under the platforms. However, one night during a thunderstorm, Shep scratched at the door to be let in and curled up on an old blanket beside the stove. The McSweeneys still had no idea from where the stray dog had come.

Dogs of the Railways

After a few years of Shep's vigil, Conductor Ed Shields talked to the undertaker and others who might know Shep's story and pieced together how Shep had come to Fort Benton. Shields discovered that Shep had belonged to a sheepherder who died and that the undertaker had shipped the body east from the Fort Benton station.

The sheepherder[1] was one of the pioneering men who lived their lives on the vast expanse of the lonely prairie and who lived with their dogs and their sheep as their companions. Shep was probably one of the collie-like sheepdogs that helped move herds across America's vast plains. A dog was often a herder's best friend on the remote plains of Montana. A single sheepdog can typically herd flocks of 80 or more sheep in their daily work and in competitive herding.[2] Sheepdogs were a breed of herding dog originally descended from pastoral dogs brought from England. Most were English shepherds or border collies. They gathered and protected the herds that grazed in the high country and open ranges. Intelligent and independent dogs could travel great distances to collect their flock for their handlers. The sheepdogs were steady, willing to please, calm, and intelligent. They could also herd other types of livestock. Their most significant characteristic was their bond with their human partner.

Ed Shields wrote a story about Shep's faithful vigil on the Great Northern Railroad that was published in *The Great Falls Tribune*. The Associated Press and United Press ran Shep's story. Ripley's "Believe It or Not" carried Shep's story in syndication. Magazine articles appeared to tell the story of Shep and his fame spread.

Admirers worldwide sent mail to Shep in volumes, and the railroad company had to assign a secretary to handle Shep's correspondence. People from all over the country made special trips to Fort Benton to see Shep. Admirers sent him presents, and sheepherders from across the globe offered to adopt him. But Shep remained a one-person dog.

The Great Northern Railroad

Railroads transformed life and economic development in Montana. The completion of the railroad to Fort Benton signaled the end of the steamboat era. Before 1880, Montana was isolated, and transportation was seasonal. It was hard to get to Montana in the summer and almost impossible in the winter. Most travelers arrived on foot and traveled by foot or horseback across the plains and mountains.

6. Shep

The original Fort Benton was the last trading post on the upper Missouri River. An important economic center for Fort Benton and a hub for water transportation, it became the "Chicago of the West" as America's most inner port city. American steam vessels could travel 2,600 miles up the river from St. Louis, a cheap way to get supplies, equipment, and people to Montana. Benton was land-locked in midsummer when the Montana River was too low to be navigable by steamboat.

Miners, merchants, farmers, and cattlemen had arrived in the 1860s hoping for faster, cheaper transportation. As the U.S. population headed west in the late 19th and early 20th century, meat was needed to supply the camps that had risen up in a rush for treasure and fortunes when gold was discovered, and men had depleted existing food supplies. Sheep and cattle were brought west to fill the need, and the Great Northern Railroad picked up thousands of sheep for shipment to the Midwest and Pacific.

The Great Northern expanded between 1891 and 1907, building an average of one new mile of the railroad every working day.[3] The Great Northern hugged the Canadian border and eventually stretched from Lake Superior in Duluth and Minneapolis–St. Paul and traveled through Montana, North Dakota, and Northern Idaho to Washington State.

The Great Northern was unique. It was built without the benefit of land grants allocated to other transcontinental railroads. James Jerome Hill was credited with the development of the Great Northern Railroad. He was known as the "empire builder" for his ability to create a prosperous business in a vacuum where none existed. Hill had 20+ years of experience with freighting, merchandising, and transportation. The empire builder had a reputation for respecting his men and knowing most of his superintendents by name.[4] It was said that once when he was traveling in a special coach, the train was blocked by heavy snowfall; he started shoveling snow himself and told the men helping him to get coffee from his coach.

Eventually, American railroads united the East and West, creating communities and links between them. Towns that sprung up along the rail lines were rough and undisciplined, but the railroad provided a vehicle for eastern towns and communities to impose their legal, economic, and social forms upon their western neighbors.

During the Great Depression, railroad and wartime economic expansion brought social and cultural transitions and changed the patterns of rural life in Benton and across the nation. People across America were often homeless or out of work. Women entered the workforce and remained there. Populations migrated from farms and towns to the cities with defense industries. People learned to cope with new social and economic problems.[5]

In hard times, dogs were not the only ones attracted to life riding the rails. A hobo culture developed across America. Human hoboes passed through railroad towns like Benton. The lure of the rails and the hope for a better future drew thousands of young people to life on the railroad. Over 250,000 teenagers left home to become hoboes on the railways in search of a better life. Known as boxcar boys and girls, they represented the hopelessness of the Depression era. The hobo culture developed with its own language and dubious charm. It was a time of dashed dreams, new hope, the fear and horrors of war, and a yearning for heroes.

Many humans struggling with their daily life challenges could identify with an itinerant hobo dog who lived his life on his own terms during tough times. By early 1941, America was preparing for war, and citizens of Benton and towns across America were anxious. Residents of the Great Plains had begun practicing blackout drills for home defense and were joining the Civil Air Patrol. Wartime brought both economic hardship and opportunity to Benton and Montana.

As America held its breath waiting for war, the story of a simple sheepdog's faithfulness and courage gave the people of Montana and across the country hope at a time when national anxiety reigned, fueled by the daily frightening and sobering news of Germany's conquests and the gathering storms of war. Shep, the endearing vagabond canine, became one of the best-known dogs in America. People all over the country looked forward to heartwarming news about Shep, a faithful dog still waiting for his partner. When the Associated Press, United Press, and international news services carried Shep's story, it ran alongside stories of Hitler bombing Polish cities while France and Britain rallied against the Third Reich.

A Vigil Ends, but a Legacy Endures

On January 12, 1942, Shep was waiting for an approaching train. The engineer blasted the steam whistle twice as the locomotive approached the station. The old dog didn't hear the whistle's blast. He

6. Shep

ran across the tracks but could not make the jump onto the depot platform and fell back on the tracks. The engineer tried the whistle again and tried to stop, but it was too late to avoid hitting Shep. Some Benton citizens suggested that after 5½ years of holding a vigil on the Great Northern, the aging Shep must have grown hard of hearing.

Days after Japan's attack on Pearl Harbor, America's most beloved dog was buried on a bluff overlooking the Great Northern depot. A town and nation mourned. City fathers and men of the Great Northern organized a funeral for Shep. School was dismissed so school children could attend the funeral. Two days after his death, hundreds of people arrived to participate. Boy Scouts acted as pallbearers and carried Shep to his gravesite overlooking the station. Two mayors spoke, and the Rev. Ralph Underwood conducted a memorial service. A Boy Scout sounded taps on his bugle. Nearly everyone in Benton attended the funeral, and thousands sent messages of sympathy to Fort Benton.

Great Northern employees erected a profile monument of Shep and built a concrete marker in his honor. The station installed a spotlight that was lit each night so passengers on evening trains could see the monument to a single loyal dog.[6]

Shep's story touched a nation at war. Millions of Americans were leaving home to fight, yet hundreds of people attended the funeral of a single dog. Shep's example of loyalty and faithfulness spoke to people's hearts and became part of the story of Fort Benton and the people of Montana. The death of Shep was a tragedy for the town and America, and word of his death spread worldwide. Fifty-two years after Shep's death, Fort Benton residents and fans of Shep from all over the world erected a bronze statue by sculptor Bob Scriver of Browning, Montana. It stands on the banks of the Missouri River in Benton City Park.

Another enduring legacy of Shep's story came from the profits of the booklet about him. Stewards and porters on the Great Northern often told the story of Shep to passengers. Shields, the Great Northern conductor, wrote a short booklet about Shep. Entitled *The Faithful Dog of the Great Northern*, it sold for 50¢ aboard westbound trains. Its popularity spread, and its proceeds eventually reached nearly $25,000. Shields then established a living memorial to Shep and created the "Hero Fund."

Shields offered it to the Montana School for the Deaf and the Blind superintendent. The children at the school came from broken homes and lonely ranches, and the school needed toys, candy, and skates for Christmas. The charity established in Shep's honor could

Dogs of the Railways

provide money for items the state legislature couldn't fund. Hoping to see something happy emerge from Shep's story, Shields directed proceeds from booklet sales to the school, money that effectively launched the Montana School for the Deaf and the Blind Foundation. Since Shep's death in 1942, the fund grew to over $100,000. Eventually, the contributions in Shep's honor provided not just Christmas gifts but a year-round program of care and therapy that might include trips to the capital, visits to dude ranches, and camp outings at Yellowstone National Park.

Faithful Shep had become Santa Claus to the children of the school. Stewart H. Beveridge and Lee Nelson told Shep's story in a book of historical fiction, *Shep: Forever Faithful*, published in 2005.

* * *

Passenger trains no longer pass through Benton, and the old depot has been torn down. In 1970, the Great Northern, along with the Northern Pacific, the Chicago, Burlington and Quincy, and Spokane Northern, merged with the Santa Fe to create the Burlington Northern Railways. In 1996, Burlington Northern merged with the Atchison, Topeka, and Santa Fe Railway to form the Burlington Northern and Santa Fe Railway.

Railroads entered the post-war period with optimism that saw an increased purchase of new locomotives, equipment, and passenger routes. But the decline in railroads that began before the war resumed afterward in favor of reliance on and enthusiasm for air travel and automobiles. The last steam locomotive was retired in the 1950s in favor of the diesel engine.

Benton, Montana, today is about an hour's drive northeast from Great Falls, Montana. It sits in a narrow valley on the west bank of the Missouri River. It's a picturesque town with tree-lined streets and shady parks. The waterfront area was designated a national historic landmark in 1961. Shep's grave sits on the north edge of Fort Benton atop the bluff overlooking the abandoned railroad station. Passenger trains no longer run, and the railroad tracks now carry only grain cars and switch engines. But the tracks still wind around the bluffs just as when Shep held vigil for his guardian, an unknown sheepherder.

On January 11, 2022, on the eightieth anniversary of Shep's death, The *Great Falls Tribune* ran a story of "The magical life and times and afterlife of Shep, Benton's famous faithful dog." The story noted that eighty years after Shep's death the world still loves Benton's faithful dog Shep for who Shep was and for all the good done in Shep's honor.[7]

A concrete obelisk memorial sits on top of the mountain with the

6. Shep

"Forever Faithful," Bob Scriver bronze statue of Shep, Fort Benton Montana, 1994 (Wikimedia).

letters SHEP. A wooden silhouette of Shep has been replaced by one of steel.[8] It stands today as a community's testament to how the love of a dog sustained them during difficult times and represents the enduring legacy of an unknown sheepherder and his dog.

7

Fala

A Raildog Rides the Funeral Train, 1945

On March 29, 1945, as a train headed for Warm Springs, Georgia, Fala, a black Scottish terrier, plopped down into one of the comfortable armchairs on the presidential Pullman car. The dog wore a silver collar that read, "I belong to the President." The chair was one of the dog's favorite spots when he traveled with Franklin Delano Roosevelt (F.D.R.). Fala, the president's dog, and the commander-in-chief went everywhere together, and they traveled in style. They rode in the luxurious 1932 specially designed railroad car, the Ferdinand Magellan, the Air Force One of its day.[1] The Ferdinand Magellan provided intense security for the wartime president. F.D.R. also liked the privacy that the unique design of the Ferdinand Magellan provided. The president contracted polio in 1921 and traveled with the assistance of a wheelchair. He wanted to conceal the extent of his lower body paralysis from the public.

Fala accompanied F.D.R. on most train trips and knew every corridor and corner of the Ferdinand Magellan—better than any guests or porters.[2] On the March 28 trip, the Roosevelt family, friends, and staffers were bound for Warm Springs, a favorite place of the president outside of Atlanta. It was a place he could relax in privacy and a secluded area in a small cottage. His staff dubbed the cottage retreat "The Little White House."

But this trip was different. On most trips to Warm Springs, F.D.R. relaxed in the Ferdinand Magellan's observation car, playing cards with his guests and enjoying a cocktail as they dropped into their armchairs for the trip and conversation.[3] On this trip, F.D.R. did not join his guests but wheeled down the corridor to bedroom C and went to sleep.[4] Roosevelt had looked tired when he boarded the train.

This would be the last train ride Fala would take with a living F.D.R.

7. Fala

The 32nd president of the United States suffered a stroke and died on April 12, 1945, in Warm Springs, Georgia. Two weeks later, the Ferdinand Magellan would again carry the president of the United States, this time in a coffin. The friends and staffers who had accompanied the weary president to Warm Springs, hoping for a time of relaxation for the tired president, instead began a plan for a presidential return home to Hyde Park, New York, a funeral, and a transition of power at a critical moment for America. The Ferdinand Magellan had become the funeral train.

At the cottage in Warm Springs, Eleanor Roosevelt and William Hassett, an assistant secretary to F.D.R., sat together before the funeral train departed. They made a list of the people invited to sit in the honored seats on the Pullman aboard the funeral train on the second leg of the trip to Hyde Park.[5] At 7:17 PM, a telegram arrived at the White House Communication Office with a list of party members to travel from Washington to Hyde Park and return.[6] Sixty-six names were on the list. Near the top of the list, which included presidential intimates, press secretaries, family, and aides, was a beloved black Scottish terrier.[7] A faithful raildog would accompany his beloved president home. As the Ferdinand Magellan rolled on, bound through a historic demonstration of national grief, the train that F.D.R. so loved carried the dog he loved on their last journey together.

* * *

It is no surprise that Fala Roosevelt makes his way into this profile of notable American raildogs. Fala's bond with the president of the United States was forged on one of the most famous railcars in history. Fala and F.D.R. spent hours together traveling by train and their bond was forged and tempered by steel rails, war, and the wounds of a nation still recovering from the Great Depression. Their bond extended until F.D.R.'s death and beyond. Fala found his home in F.D.R.'s heart and on a famous rail car.

A presidential pooch may seem more likely to be a pampered celebrity than a vagabond raildog. Fala fit the raildog profile: rugged individualist, charismatic, with a sense of mischief and adventure, and an appetite for cajoling fellow rail travelers out of treats. But Fala was more than just a companion pet to an important man. He was one of the most influential presidential pets in American history. His bond with Franklin Delano Roosevelt supported the president as he led the United States through some of the nation's most significant challenges, war, and political drama.

Dogs of the Railways

Franklin Roosevelt's cousin Margaret "Daisy" Suckley presented Fala to Roosevelt as a gift from Mrs. Augustus Kellogg of Connecticut. F.D.R. renamed the pup Fala to honor one of his ancestors.[8] Fala was born in 1940, a year in which America was holding its collective breath with the possibility of entering World War II. War waged on in Europe, and Adolf Hitler prepared to attack England by air after invading France. While America was divided on the war, with some condemning the war as "Europe's War," a small black Scottish terrier arrived at the White House armed with a set of tricks. He knew on command to sit up, roll over, and jump. He could curl his lip into a smile. He wowed visitors and V.I.P.s when he stood at attention on his hind legs when the national anthem played.[9] Fala remained a skilled and enthusiastic performer throughout his life and often entertained White House visitors with his shenanigans.

The president himself fed Fala. The presidential breakfast tray always featured a bone for Fala, and the First Dog got a hearty dinner every night but would still beg for food from the White House staff. Fala and his routines were so appealing that he became sick from all the treats he coaxed out of his admirers. Fala's goodies-for-tricks campaign soon resulted in a presidential decree prohibiting feeding the presidential pup any extra food. The First Dog had 24-hour access to the commander-in-chief and enjoyed posh accommodations. Fala slept on a special chair at the foot of F.D.R.'s bed.

As a Scottish terrier, Fala sported the famous Scottie silhouette and persona, a short-legged but substantial terrier with distinctive fur on the beard, legs, and lower body, erect ears, and tail, alert for signs of fun.[10] Like most of his breed, he was independent and confident; when the occasion called for it, he could appear dignified.

Fala performed a full repertoire of tricks but was at his best when ad-libbing. Fala gnawed on Roosevelt's trouser cuffs for attention if he felt it necessary or tossed a bone around. Fala wagged his tail for everyone but had some particular favorites. When Admiral McIntire, a favorite friend of Fala, came into the room, Fala put his head down on the floor sideways, then turned over on his back, and the admiral would respond by giving Fala a belly rub.[11]

Fala and F.D.R. were a love match from the start. The president loved most animals, but Fala captured his heart. He had Fala's pen placed outside where he could watch the Scottish terrier race around on the grounds. Fala and F.D.R. both loved the water. Fala had some fun on one fishing trip they enjoyed together near Florida. Fala saw that as the

7. Fala

fish were caught, they would flip-flop as they were thrown into a pile on the deck. Fala joined in, started to flip-flop like the fish, and continued doing that for several days on the trip.[12]

Fala accompanied Roosevelt almost everywhere, from the Oval Office to travels for official state visits. The presidential pooch had a regular appointment with the leader of the free world during the day in his office before they went back to the big house at the end of the day. However, Fala was not permitted to attend cabinet meetings, so he would not lick ankles or brush against legs during critical discussions.[13]

The Scottish terrier was a seasoned traveler and divided his time between the White House, the president's home in Hyde Park, and Warm Springs, Georgia, where F.D.R. often enjoyed relaxation time and some privacy he could not get in Washington. Fala was F.D.R.'s travel companion, and he could be seen at the president's side on long and short train, car and boat trips. F.D.R. and Fala spent some of their most pleasurable time together on the rails. Roosevelt made over 40 trips to Warm Springs, and Fala was with him on most of them.[14] On the train and at home, Fala bunked with the president on their travels; where the commander-in-chief went, Fala did too.

Fala was present at critical moments in history. In the summer of 1941, he traveled with the president on F.D.R.'s yacht the *Potomac*, on the way to the U.S.S. *Augusta*, a Navy ship, and then on to the Atlantic Charter Conference in Newfoundland, where he met Prime Minister Winston Churchill. While there, Fala performed a repertoire of his tricks for Churchill to snag a treat from the prime minister. After the meeting, Fala looked directly into the camera as a photo captured the image of the members of the historic meeting—two world leaders, admirals, officers, aides, their entourages, and a Scottish terrier.[15]

The presidential pooch kept a busy schedule. He inspected defense plants with F.D.R. and visited the president of Mexico. In 1944, Fala traveled to the Quebec conferences with the president.[16]

The busy Scottie helped the war effort when America entered World War II. He became a private and served as president of Barkers for Britain, a dog chapter of the Bundles for Britain organization created to collect donated supplies for the United Kingdom. The dog chapter, Barkers for Britain, allowed dog lovers to support the war effort. New members were awarded a Barkers for Britain collar tag. Fala served as president and wore Tag #1.[17]

Fala caused uproar on the ship U.S.S. *Tuscaloosa* in the West Indies on one of their travels. The sailors tried to cool off on a hot day by stretching out on the ship's deck with their bare feet lined up. It was just too tempting for Fala, who moved down the line, licking and tickling the sailors' feet. Quite the brouhaha occurred on deck.[18]

In her book, *F.D.R., My Boss*, Grace Tully reported that Fala sulked if he was not taken on a presidential trip. He disrupted the schedule of the January 1941 inauguration schedule as Roosevelt was preparing to take the oath of office for a third term, bounding into the car's back seat, taking the space reserved for the president, Senator Barkley, and Speaker Rayburn. When Fala dug in and refused to move, a Secret Service agent had to intervene and relocate the insulted Scottie.[19]

Fala became so popular in the White House that he received thousands of pieces of fan mail, some from animals. The famous pooch became a movie star when two movies were made about his life at the White House and Hyde Park.

"He's Not Been the Same Dog Since"

The connection between presidents and dogs is personal and public, and a presidential pup can become a political operative. Fala became a valuable asset to F.D.R. in a heated political campaign. His 1944 presidential campaign was losing momentum, and Fala became the target of a political attack against F.D.R. On a trip to the Aleutian Islands, a rumor started that Fala had been accidentally left behind on a Navy destroyer, and F.D.R. had to retrieve the presidential canine. Although the story about Fala being left behind proved false, Representative Howard Knutson of Minnesota accused Roosevelt of extravagance during a congressional debate, claiming F.D.R. sent a Navy destroyer to the Aleutian Islands to rescue the Scottish terrier.

On September 23, 1944, during a campaign dinner with the International Brotherhood of Teamsters union, F.D.R. defended Fala's honor. Roosevelt said his opponents used Fala as an excuse to attack the president. Roosevelt suggested that Republican critics had circulated a story of his using 20 million dollars taxpayer dollars to go back and pick up the dog. He declared that his critics ruined the reputation of a defenseless dog to distract Americans from other serious national issues. He spoke to a national radio audience of millions in what would become known as "The Fala Speech":

> These Republican leaders have not been content to make personal attacks on me, or my wife, or on my sons. No, not content with that they now include

my little dog, Fala. Well, of course, I don't resent attacks, and my family don't resent attacks, but Fala does resent them. You know, you know, Fala is Scotch, and being a Scottie, as soon as he learned that the Republican fiction-writers in Congress and out had concocted a story that I had left him behind on the Aleutian Islands and had sent a destroyer back to find him— at a cost to the taxpayers of two or three, or eight or twenty million dollars—his Scotch soul was furious. He has not been the same dog since. I am accustomed to hearing malicious falsehoods about myself.... But I think I have a right to resent, to object, to libelous statements about my dog.[20]

The Fala speech turned the campaign around. The public, media, and the audience loved it. In her book, *No Ordinary Time: Franklin and Eleanor Roosevelt: The Home Front in World War II*, Doris Kearns Goodwin wrote, "The audience went wild, laughing and cheering and calling for more. And the laughter carried beyond the banquet hall; it reverberated in living rooms and kitchens throughout the country, where people were listening to the speech on their radios.

The Fala bit was so funny, one reporter observed, that 'even the stoniest of Republican faces cracked a smile.'"[21]

Fala's appeal worked on the national audience. Fala's soft and charming image softened any hard edge of the president's attack on his critics. Fala took the hit as the victim, making the accusers seem ridiculous, using humor and pathos.[22]

An "Informer" Rides the Ferdinand Magellan

For four days in April 1945, F.D.R. took his final rail journey as the Ferdinand Magellan lumbered on its funeral journey, passing crowds of grief-stricken Americans along the tracks. The new President Harry Truman and his wife, Bess, were on board to accompany Roosevelt's body to Hyde Park.

The funeral train carried the dead president's casket, a tattered nation's hope, and inconsolable grief. The casket rode back to Hyde Park in another Pullman car because the bulletproof windows of the Magellan could not be removed to fit the casket. The train was converted so the coffin could be seen by the public, who lined a thousand miles of tracks carrying the dead president from Warm Spring to Washington and then Hyde Park. Aboard the funeral train were most of the U.S. government, one dead president and one live one, their families, cabinet members, presidential staff leaders of both houses of Congress, the nine justices of the Supreme Court, and one Scottish terrier.[23]

Eleanor rode in the Magellan with Fala and others. The presidential car rode the second car from the rear for the first time.[24] Fala did not ride by the president's side but instead accompanied the first lady. In her journal, Daisy Suckley wrote of Fala, "Dear little Fala knows something is wrong. He is depressed. He wanders around—in the press car, he feels at home, but he knows his master is not here."[25] For the duration of the train's trip, Fala would not go into the president's bedroom.[26]

The Ferdinand Magellan

When the United States entered World War II, F.D.R. needed a train to provide comfortable accommodations, increased privacy and security, and unique accommodations for his wheelchair. The Ferdinand Magellan was modified for the president's needs. Its official name was the Ferdinand Magellan, but the rolling White House was code-named "U.S. Car Number 1." The name Ferdinand Magellan did not appear on the car's sides for security reasons, although its unique design made it difficult to disguise. The car usually was the last car on the train with an accompanying car, the Conneaut.

Called "the Air Force One of its Day"[27] by *Architectural Digest*, the presidential rail car had nickel-steel armor and 3-inch-thick bullet-resistant windows. The car weighed 142 tons—almost double the weight of the standard 80-ton Pullman car. It was the heaviest passenger train built in the U.S.[28] The rolling White House was a 10-room car. The Magellan fleet included sleeping and office cars for White House staff, an Army medical car, and a communications car nicknamed "the crate." The presidential limousine and Secret Service Cadillacs were transported in a special garage car. Two locomotives pulled it.[29] The Magellan contained a presidential suite with two separate bedrooms for Franklin and Eleanor Roosevelt, two guest rooms, a dining and conference room, and an observation lounge. The rear platform's microphone and loudspeakers were used in whistle stop tours. Security features included two escape hatches, sides, floor, and back door sheathed in armor plating. It was a rolling fortress.[30]

Roosevelt had traveled 50,000 miles on the presidential train during his 12-year presidency,[31] most trips with Fala by his side. F.D.R. was thrilled each time he traveled in the "rolling White House." He preferred a ride at a leisurely 30 mph pace that didn't jolt his wheelchair.[32] The Magellan technically belonged to the Association of American Railroads, but it was always assumed to be the president's car.

7. Fala

He had christened his special rail car himself in December 1942, inspecting the car from end to end and giving it his approval. William Hassett recalled in his autobiography that the christening of the car occurred a short time after the bombing of Pearl Harbor, and F.D.R. still had not grown accustomed to the new concern for safety and security in wartime.[33] Daisy Suckley wrote about Fala's reaction to the new car's comforts in her diary: "Great excitement over the new car. The decoration is grey-blue and tan—very nice. Fala tried all the chairs, and he decided he liked the one with the arms upholstered."[34]

In his book *FDR's Funeral Train*, Robert Klara described the tight security precautions taken in advance of the president's train. Railroad police removed posts at overpasses and junctions. Plainclothes officers established a presence at stations along the route, alert for suspicious persons. Track gangs walked every mile of track to check for broken rails and locking switches on the route that the president's train would travel.[35]

Despite the extensive security precautions, Fala could be counted on to blow Roosevelt's cover. The Secret Service gave Fala the code name "The Informer" since they knew that Fala accompanied F.D.R. everywhere. Occasionally, the "Informer" Fala would convince an aide to take him out for a walk at a stop. The security precautions would be useless, and the president's location on the Ferdinand Magellan was revealed.[36]

The Magellan had the first right of way wherever it traveled, and railroad companies kept other traffic at least 30 minutes away in either direction. After its journey as the funeral train, the Magellan served four presidents and became the only passenger rail car designated a national historic landmark.[37]

"Run Slow, Run Silent"

As the funeral train rolled on its somber trip, the engineers adhered to the orders "run slow, run silent," and the train ran no faster than 25 miles per hour. The First Lady requested the slow speed with respect and safety in mind due to all the people along the tracks. The somber grieving public stood along the route in tiny depots, at crossings, on sides, often in the middle of nowhere. Grace Tully wrote:

> In each hamlet and each city on the route, crowds of mourning Americans, and friends, lined the tracks unmindful of heat or chill, sunlight or darkness, as they paid this parting tribute. Many were singing hymns, all were

bareheaded, and many were weeping. Aboard the train, there was quiet and darkness; affected alike were the members of the White House staff and the train attendants, grieved beyond words.[38]

At a stop on the funeral route, a presidential valet gave Fala some fresh air. The little dog bounded off the train, and photographers' lights flashed as Fala sniffed his way through hordes of ankles. The next day the *Atlanta* magazine reported that the little dog "wagged his tail in response to the sympathetic response of the bystanders."[39]

Later, in the funeral procession, when Eleanor, Grace Tully, Laura Delano, and Daisy Suckley rode in the sedan that followed the hearse, Fala was lying at their feet. The *New York Times* reported, "Fala, who was at Mrs. Roosevelt's feet, seemed to know something was wrong and perhaps sensing what it was."[40] At F.D.R.'s funeral on April 15, 1945, "the West Point cadets raised their rifles and fired three volleys. After each volley [Eleanor's friend Trude Lash] noted that Fala barked, a child whimpered, and it was over."[41]

General Eisenhower visited Roosevelt's estate to lay a wreath. Eleanor Roosevelt wrote in her autobiography that "when Fala heard the sirens of the police escort accompanying Eisenhower, Fala's legs straightened out, his ears pricked up and I knew he expected to see his master coming down the drive."[42]

"Fala Never Forgot"

A year before he died, F.D.R. had told Grace Tully, his secretary, that if anything happened to him, she should get Fala because he was sure Eleanor would be too busy to look after the active terrier. While they lived at the White House, Eleanor Roosevelt disapproved of having a dog live there, but Eleanor asked Daisy to return Fala to her after the president's death. Fala lived the rest of his life in retirement with Eleanor.[43] She had grown fond of the black terrier, perhaps through an understanding of shared grief. Eleanor wrote:

> It was Fala, my husband's little dog, who never really readjusted.... When we were living in the cottage, Fala always lay near the dining-room door to watch both entrances just as he did when his master was there. Franklin would often decide to go somewhere, and Fala had to watch both entrances to be ready to spring up and join the party on short notice.[44]

Fala lived another seven years with Eleanor at Hyde Park. He enjoyed a retirement filled with country air, chasing squirrels and even

7. Fala

cats, and playing with F.D.R.'s grandson. Fala would be exhausted and enjoy a sound sleep with his feet in the air.

Fala died in 1952 and was buried on April 5, 1952, next to the sundial in the Hyde Park Rose Garden, not far from the graves of Mr. and Mrs. Roosevelt. He would have been 12 years old on his birthday.[45] His hair had turned grey, and he was deaf. The *Times* called him the "elder statesmen of dogs who sat at the feet of some of the most important men."[46]

Today Fala sits memorialized in a sculpture of F.D.R. and Fala at the Franklin Delano Roosevelt Memorial between the Lincoln and Jefferson Memorials in Washington, D.C. The statues of Franklin Roosevelt and Fala were sculpted by Neil Estern of Brooklyn Heights, New York. At the request of Michigan Senator Carl Levin, a Franklin Delano Roosevelt Commission member, Estern agreed to add Fala, not "to be frivolous but rather to portray the human side of a great man."[47]

The Magellan is exhibited at the Gold Coast Railroad Museum in Miami.

But Fala's raildog story doesn't end there. Even after his death, Fala is part of a mystery surrounding one of the most famous railroad cars in history and the possible secrets beneath Grand Central Station Track 61. Some say Fala's spirit endures and still lingers near this railroad platform in New York, perhaps hoping to recapture the magic of a ride on the Magellan and a stay with his beloved F.D.R.

Track 61, a Grand Central Secret Platform, and a Fala Ghost Story

As with many myths and legends, the Fala story has some basis. A contemporary Fala legend links to speculation that F.D.R. used a secret Track 61 to arrive discreetly at the Waldorf Astoria in New York City to conceal that he used a wheelchair due to the paralysis of his lower body he contracted in 1921 when he had polio.

Grand Central Station had taken a decade to build. As part of the station's unique magnificent architecture, the tracks dropped below grade level, and structures were built over the Grand Central Station's track, one of which was the superb Waldorf Astoria Hotel. The hotel encompasses an entire Midtown block of mid–Manhattan bounded by Park and Lexington Avenues and 59th and 50th Streets. The platform hosted so many presidents it became known as the presidential platform and even the F.D.R. train station.⁴⁸ Secrecy surrounded the private car. Since the platform was designed to conceal and provide security for the president, it's not surprising that the public knew little about its existence, and proof of it remained elusive.⁴⁹ A reported myth about F.D.R. and Track 61 in New York City was that his personal railcar sat abandoned at the track since 1945.⁵⁰

At its opening, the Waldorf had heralded its ability to accommodate high-profile guests with private train cars. Some say that the blue baggage car with an extra-wide door sat on Track 63 and that the Waldorf used to carry Roosevelt's Pierce Arrow car. An elevator and adjacent stairway connected a platform at Track 61 outside the hotel at 49th Street. Some speculate that the president used the platform to arrive unseen at the hotel at least once and possibly more often to conceal his wheelchair from the public. Accounts of Track 61 and Roosevelt's use of it to access the Waldorf are sketchy, and attempts to confirm that F.D.R. used the platform have met with limited success.⁵¹

Kurt Schlichting reported, "When Roosevelt stayed at the hotel, he used the train platform. His aides could then carry the president through a door and take the elevator directly to his room."⁵² William D. Middleton, writing in his 1977 book, *Grand Central, the World's Greatest Railway Terminal*, said that while campaigning in 1944, F.D.R. "gave a foreign policy address at the Waldorf and then descended into the 'basement' to the presidential rail car to journey home to Hyde Park."⁵³ In an April 2002 article in *Trains* magazine, "Train Myths and Legends," Karl Zimmerman profiled a Who's Who of Grand Central's secret Track 61. Zimmerman found it plausible that F.D.R. used Track 61 since it represented a short trip up the Hudson to Hyde Park, where there was a private car siding.⁵⁴ One documented use by F.D.R. of the Waldorf siding was October 21, 1944, when F.D.R. disembarked from the Magellan at the Brooklyn Army Terminal and several other locations before going to the Waldorf.

Another part of the conjecture is that Roosevelt would board his limousine, the Pierce Arrow, right on the platform and then ride up the freight elevator in it into the Waldorf garage. The automobile often was carried by rail. This theory does not appear valid since the car, which had been sitting on Track 61 all these years, is now believed to be baggage car MNCW #002. It also is doubtful because it would have taken quite a bit of maneuvering to fit a Pierce Arrow limousine through its doors. Despite the 1944 departure being Roosevelt's only documented use of the track, the late president became synonymous with Track 61, often referred to as the "presidential siding."⁵⁵

7. Fala

A Fala railroad ghost story extends the Track 61 legend still further. The private track is closed now, but the underground caverns of Grand Central were said to have a ghostly canine visitor. The ghost story's logic goes that Fala frequently made the trip with F.D.R. to Hyde Park, so it's likely Fala went with the president when F.D.R. slipped into the Waldorf at the underground station. Fala would be nearby when F.D.R. traveled to the Waldorf. Fala's barks usually announced the presence of the chief and would be a sure sign Roosevelt was present. Some workers at the underground station reportedly claimed they still saw Fala's ghost wandering the station platform, searching for F.D.R. in Grand Central's below-ground caverns late at night. Phil Shoenberg, a New York historian and founder of Ghost Tours of New York, claimed Fala still appears in Grand Central looking and waiting for F.D.R. The late presidential pup was reported to be spotted late at night by people working below the Waldorf near the underground station. Fala's ghost story was the most popular story on Shoenberg's ghost tour.[56]

It may be just like the lively Scottish terrier to be the star of a railroad ghost story. A mixture of fact and urban myth, the stories of Fala, F.D.R., and the Magellan continue to be part of the conversation for those fascinated with trains, dogs, and the human-animal bond. Throw in a canine ghost story, and the combination is irresistible.

Fala is not the first beloved dog to enjoy a ghostly legacy. Folklore is rich with canine ghost tales. More than half of Americans surveyed by a 2018 *Economist* poll said they believe in ghosts,[57] and a 2015 *Psychology Today* poll found that 84 percent of bereaved pet owners believed that past pets had visited them at least for a second.[58]

Whatever the story's veracity, many find it fun and touching to think of the faithful little terrier still wandering about the train station, yearning and looking for F.D.R. on the railroad they both loved so much.

Fala's Legacy

Canine specter or mere mortal superstar, Fala ranks as one of the most memorable raildogs. Fala's role in F.D.R.'s presidency has unique features in American history. Even though Fala came to F.D.R. when Roosevelt was already president, Fala was discussed ten times in presidential press conferences, mentioned 31 times in the *New York Times*, and starred in a 1942 movie. Fala's popularity made it possible

Dogs of the Railways

for Roosevelt to mention his dog frequently, and the little black Scottie became a resource for stories of whimsy and warmth. Fala was a sidekick, a mascot for the president, and a public figure in his own right.[59]

As recognized by anyone who has had a trusted dog by their side during significant challenges and tragedy, a profound relationship develops with that dog and exceptional communication and connection. The spirited Scottie was the dog of a president who traveled in style. Perhaps it was only Fala to whom the president of the United States confided some of his innermost secrets and fears.

The steel rails under an historic rail car forged his bond with the commander-in-chief as he traveled everywhere with the president. Fala facilitated F.D.R.'s communication with the public during wartime and even encouraged people to make sacrifices during the war effort. The White House released information that Fala had given up his rubber toys and donated them as part of a style. As F.D.R. wrestled with the war and the fate of a nation, faithful Fala was by his side. Dogs can help humans handle the stress of crisis and enormous responsibility. Fala helped provide a sense of normalcy and comic relief to the commander-in-chief during a time of significant challenges. Fala helped a nation endure World War II and then mourn the loss of its leader at a pivotal moment in history. A Scottish terrier standing at attention for the national anthem may well have helped to heal a frightened nation's trauma.

President Franklin D. Roosevelt with Fala by his side on Ferdinand Magellan, April 20, 1943 (National Museum of the U.S. Navy).

7. Fala

Bronze sculpture by Neil Estern of Franklin Delano Roosevelt (in his wheelchair) and his dog Fala at the Franklin Delano Roosevelt Memorial, Washington, between 1997 and 2006 (Library of Congress via Wikimedia Commons).

Fala's image and antics humanized the president and relieved weary Americans from war's terrors. Fala was the nation's dog, part of the collective American family. F.D.R. led the country through some of its darkest hours and left behind a grieving nation. Fala grieved along with them. Fala became a symbol of national mourning and helped a country grieve the loss of the leader who had guided the country through fear and war. The nation watched Fala, still grieving, go on, and the country and its new president could go on, too.

Perhaps our understanding of grief and longing for those we have lost, or maybe the memory of a small dog's grief for a great man, explains why a legend surfaced that Fala's ghost occasionally wanders Track 61 under the Waldorf. That Fala still roams the tracks below the hotel is testimony to the continuing interest in a little dog who symbolizes love and devotion for his human guardian and a raildog whose

Dogs of the Railways

legend endures. What is true is that Fala continues in our conversation and memory and indeed deserves a place in our gallery of famous raildogs who found a family and belonging on the railroad. Perhaps the railroad was one of the places where a president and a raildog had been happiest.

8

Brownie

The Victorville, California, Railroad Station Mascot, 1943–1945

It's an iconic drive down Route 66 into California's high desert. When the road runs through the town center in Victorville, the California Route 66 Museum comes into view. The museum sits across the street from the transit center, a modern facility that used to be the old railroad depot. In a fenced area in the Route 66 Museum parking lot, visitors find a tombstone with the inscription:

> "Brownie a Railroad Dog"
> A Friend and a Pal
> 1945[1]

Although the simple grave marker can be easy to miss, the memorial to Brownie and his story are favorite roadside attractions for pilgrims on the historic Route 66. Brownie's memorial is a testament to the enduring power of friendship. The tale of a faithful raildog like Brownie still resonates—the memory of a dog who spread cheer and comfort to soldiers in World War II.[2]

Brownie was an injured, mixed-breed dog who wandered into the Victorville train station and found compassion, family, and kindness. He became a member of the railroad family and part of the story of a high desert railroad town.

In 1943, he appeared, bruised and bleeding at the Victorville train station, the apparent victim of an encounter with a passing automobile. Since he had no collar, no one could be sure where he came from or how old he was, but it was clear that the stray dog needed help. The night telegraph operator at the rail station fed the dog a pan of warm milk, gave him a bed near the warm stove at the rail station, and nursed the dog back to health. The tan dog became a permanent 24-hour resident of the station.[3]

* * *

The rail workers called him Brownie, named for his color. He appeared to be a mixed breed of terrier and pit bull. Brownie became a

Dogs of the Railways

raildog; he spent his life greeting depot workers and inspecting trains. He became part of the railroad family and a friend to the railroad workers.

Brownie was suspicious of human affection at first, but he learned to love the workers and passengers of the railroad, and he showed it. He greeted depot workers, announced every train coming in from the Cajon Pass, and welcomed soldiers coming home from World War II at the Victorville station. The people of Victorville agreed that he was a friendly dog and a faithful friend to the railroad workers.

Times were tough in Victorville, like the rest of America. The war was raging, and American families rationed meat. Still, railroad workers saved scraps from their meals at home and brought and fed them to the hungry dog.[4] Passing train crews would feed the dog by throwing meat cooked on the caboose stove out the door of the moving train. When Brownie became ill, the railroad workers contributed money to pay for a veterinary visit.

Shirley Davisson's father was a railroad man. She remembered Brownie as a small, friendly, tan dog. She said everyone stopped and played with Brownie, and he was at the station 24 hours a day.[5] Brownie loved his human friends but wasn't as fond of other canines. He wasn't one to share his newfound territory and would chase passengers' dogs out of the station back onto the train.[6]

The town of Victorville grew up around the railroad, and the railroad was the heart of the village as it grew. Victorville was named for California Southern Railroad General Manager Jacob Nash Victor.[7] It was founded as a railroad town in 1895 when the original telegraph railroad station was built northwest of the narrows of the Mojave River. The town's name was changed to the current one in 1901 by the U.S. Post Office to avoid confusion with a town of the same name in Colorado.[8] It is located in Victor Valley in San Bernardino County, California.

Victorville was incorporated in 1962. Good land and water created a suitable environment for the development of agriculture. When large deposits of limestone and granite were discovered, the cement manufacturing business became the main economic driver for the Victor Valley.[9] The town is home to the former George Air Force Base, built in 1941, now known as the Southern California Logistics Airport.

The original train depot where Brownie first found his home burned down in 1983. The Victorville station now consists of a platform located southeast of the Victor Valley Transportation Center. Amtrak's service to the town began in 1990 and has continued since 1994 with the *Southwest Chief*. A revitalization project started in 1995 in the 10 square blocks along Historic Route 66. Demolition of hazardous and dilapidated buildings began. Old Town and the architecture were designed to reflect a contemporary take on the city's historic Route 66 heritage and preserve the architecture and history of the original train station. Projects included the Veteran's Memorial on Seventh Street and Forrest Avenue, the Route 66 Museum, the Transportation Center, and the Old Victor School.

A Raildog Remembered on Route 66

Brownie was run over and killed by a train in 1945. He received a hero's burial. The railroad employees so adored Brownie that they "placed him in a typewriter box and found a shady place under a Cottonwood tree" until they could plan a more proper burial. The workers then pooled their money together and bought Brownie a black headstone.[10] Brownie's memorial is a simple tribute to the railroad men's affection for the dog they loved who returned their affection. The city planners moved the grave and marker from Forrest Park to the Route 66 Museum, where it now stands.[11] Brownie found his final resting place along Route 66, one of the most famous roads in America. Route 66 is a fitting place to tell Brownie's story. The renowned road runs through the center of town. Brownie and his tombstone still draw tourists who travel Route 66 searching for nostalgia from a bygone era. Touring the Route 66 Museum, they discover the dog's grave and learn how the rail workers who honored him considered him a friend and a railroad dog.

In the *Grapes of Wrath,* John Steinbeck described the famous road.[12] For Steinbeck, the route was the road of flight, a symbol of comfort and hardship. Route 66 symbolized the renewed spirit of optimism that pervaded the country after an economic catastrophe and global war. This sense of optimism symbolized hope and forward movement for a generation and remains an iconic American road.

A portion of Route 66 provided a transportation corridor through Victorville. When the national highway system was established in 1926, U.S. Route 66 was one of the main links between Chicago and California. Seventh Street and D Street in Victorville were part of the national highway until Interstate 15 was constructed.[13] It reminded travelers of an exciting past when the country was developed for long-distance car travel. Often called "the Main Street of America," it linked a remote and under populated region with two vital twentieth-century cities, Chicago and Los Angeles. It had stimulated the most comprehensive westward movement, and economic growth in U.S. history.[14] By 1970, nearly all of the original

Route 66 was bypassed by a modern four-lane highway. The outdated, poorly maintained vestiges of U.S. 66 were replaced in October 1984, when its final section was bypassed by Interstate 40 at Williams, Arizona.

Route 66 and many points of interest were familiar landmarks when a new generation of postwar motorists hit the road in 1960. Today it's a place where an entire town honors the memory of a small dog who found kindness in a town and returned the favor with friendship and a legacy as a friend and a pal.

More California Raildogs

Brownie wasn't the first dog to find a home and celebrity on a California railroad. Tuolumne County, the Sierra Railway, and the Sierra Nevada region boast some memorable raildogs of years past. The Sierra Railway connected Sonora, Jamestown, and the towns of Tuolumne and Standard. It is directly related to the Santa Fe and Southern Pacific railroads in Oakdale, with access to the national rail network.[15]

Tuolumne County is in the foothills of the Sierra Nevada mountains. In 1848, gold was discovered and brought by prospectors who founded towns like Jamestown and Sonora. Later, forests, cattle ranches, and apple orchards became part of the economy.[16] The Sierra Railway in Jamestown, California, is located on the Highway 108/49 corridor.

The Gold Rush of 1848 began in Jamestown. In 1898, a stray dog named Hobo arrived in Jamestown with Station Agent F.T. Boyd and found a home at the train station.[17] Hobo liked the railroad men but was known as a wanderer. He might hop a train, travel up the rails, and return to Jamestown when he decided the time was right. Hobo relocated to Sugar Pine or Strawberry each year to spend the summer months, returning each fall to Jamestown. The entire village adopted Hobo, and he was fed and cared for by the many community members.[18]

Another well-known dog named Bob started riding stagecoaches that ran between Sonora, California, and Milton as a companion to the stagecoach drivers. When the railroad replaced stagecoaches, Bob changed with the times. He then hopped aboard a train to Stockton. He returned to Stockton on a hack, where he was cared for by the hack men of Stockton.

Bummer, another California raildog, was a shepherd dog who

8. Brownie

lived above Sonora with rancher Joseph Barron. Besides his ranch hand duties, Bummer fetched the daily paper. Rain or shine, Bummer made his way to the Black Oak Station each night and awaited the arrival of the mail train. He retrieved the paper from the express messenger and would hurry home to deliver it to Joseph Barron.[19] Bummer's career almost ended when he chased a squirrel across the train tracks and derailed a small motor rail car. Badly injured, he crawled home and was nursed back to health by Barron.

The railroads were part of the destiny of California as America changed and new commerce and communities erupted over the high desert landscape. The people of California built their towns around the railroad. The history of towns began with the railroad, and the memory of Brownie the raildog and the other raildogs of the high desert towns were as much a part of that history as the railroad itself. Today the memory of these raildogs' faithfulness, family, and friendship endure on the famous American road, Route 66, in stories and the hearts of the men and women who love the railroads and the spirit of the California raildogs who hopped on board.

9

Railroad K9 Patrols
Guardians of the Railways, 2022

A group of contemporary raildogs find a home and purpose as working dogs on modern railroads. They too have become part of the railroad family.

These guardians of the rails show up for duty laser-focused. Theirs is a serious business. They patrol America's trains and railroad structures 24 hours a day, seven days a week. Working alongside their human partners, they save lives and help stop the spread of dangerous substances and terror threats. These canines train in real-world environments and scenarios and connect to their communities as valued members of law enforcement. Some of these guardians of the railroads become celebrities, have social media accounts, and win national awards. They are beloved members of the railroad family. Guardians of America's railways came on board to serve and protect. Along the way, they found purpose, family and home.

* * *

In 2021, the Metropolitan Transportation Authority (MTA) canine unit was honored as top dogs at the Stephen and Christine Schwarzman Animal Medical Center's (AMC)[1] Top Dog Gala. The Top Dog Award is presented to a group of working dogs in honor of their commendable service.

> As one of the largest canine explosive detection forces in the nation, the MTA Police Department Canine Unit serves a critical role in protecting the Metro-North Rail Road, Long Island Railroad, Staten Island Railway, and other transportation facilities and terminals each and every day."[2] "We are honored that the Schwarzman Animal Medical Center recognized our canine unit at their *Top Dog Event*," said MTA Police Officer Giselle Gil. "It means a lot to us too. It's more than a handler and dog relationship; they are part of our family, and we have a very special bond."[3]

9. Railroad K9 Patrols

The Metropolitan Transportation Authority is North America's largest transportation network. It includes six agencies: MTA New York City Transit, MTA Bus Company, MTA Long Island Rail Road, MTA Metro-North Railroad, MTA Bridges and Tunnels, and MTA Construction and Development. The MTA serves over 15 million people in a 5,000-square-mile area from New York through Long Island, southern New York State, and Connecticut. It has more commuter rail cars than all other U.S. transit systems combined. Among commuters to New York City's central business districts, 80 percent use transit.[4] The MTA Police Department patrols the trains, stations, tracks, and yards of the Long Island Rail Road, Metro-North Railroad, and Staten Island Railway. The MTA Police Department's Canine Unit was established in 2002 to protect customers from terrorism and other criminal acts and help reduce railroad service disruptions by expediting inspections of unattended packages.[5]

In 2021, the MTA Police Department Canine Unit had 36 teams working to deter terrorism and prevent crime.[6] It's an extensive territory covering 114 New York and Connecticut counties. The MTA K9 unit supports the MTA's safety program with unique canine talents.

An elite force, only about one in 30 canines tested qualifies to join the MTA's canine explosives task force. The task force is one of the largest in the United States. The MTA's canine unit dogs are German shepherds, or shepherd/Belgian shepherd mixes, and are usually about a year and a half old. The K9s are named in honor of fallen officers, firefighters, and members of the armed forces.[7]

The dogs train at a state-of-the-art 72-acre training facility in Dutchess County, New York, with outdoor and indoor training grounds that provide the MTA Police with unlimited scenarios to teach, drill and test the dogs. The mass transit–specific training center includes 26 indoor/outdoor kennels, on-site veterinary rooms, obstacle courses, classrooms, and real-world simulated training fields, including train cars, railroad tracks, platforms, buses, and signaled crossings.[8] The training center allows the trainees to drill on unlimited scenarios for the K9 officers.[9] The MTA Police Department Premier Canine Training Center opened in 2015 to provide this extensive training.

At the opening of the center, MTA Chairman and CEO Thomas F. Prendergast noted, "Our top priority at the MTA is ensuring public safety. In our post–9/11 world, the MTAPD's specialized Canine Unit is a crucial component of the MTA's overall security strategy."[10] The MTAPD Chief of Police Michael Coan said, "Everything about this sophisticated, 17,000-square-foot facility was designed to train dogs to meet the unique demands of patrolling the MTA's railroads, stations, subways, platforms, and buses, making it the only state-of-the art 'mass transit' specific canine training center in the nation."[11]

The roles of K9 railway officers include various functions depending on the community and the railroad. In most cases, they provide a psychological and physical deterrent to threats to people and property. Canines can do in minutes what can take hours for humans to do when searching for explosives or other evidence in crimes. Their powerful sense of smell, which can be thousands of times stronger than humans, allows them to detect explosives and follow a scent trail untraceable to human staff, even breaking down specific scents. The MTA Police Department has a large mass-transit canine explosives detection force, with multiple dogs in service at any time.[12] The dogs begin training at one year old and work until age 5 to 9 when their partners' families usually adopt them.[13]

In addition to their training, the fundamental tool that makes railway police dogs effective in their role is their human-animal bond with their two-legged partner. It is that bond that can save a life. Most K9 officers go home with their human officer at the end of their shift and live as companion dogs during off-duty hours. In addition to policing skills, the law enforcement dog must learn socialization and acceptable behavior at home, and this integrative process is key to the K9 officers' development.

How Raildog Officers Joined the Railroad Police

As raildogs became part of the railroad law enforcement family, their roles evolved in response to changing times. Dogs made trustworthy and loyal partners to the human railroad police. The dogs impressed nefarious sorts and protected railroad workers and passengers and equipment. The addition of the K9 team helped make the railroad police officers some of the most capable law enforcement professionals in the United States.[14]

As the railroads grew across America, crime traveled along with them. When the railroads needed security, they turned to detectives and special agents. Allan Pinkerton established the National Detective Agency and the first railroad private detective firm. Eventually, rail corporations saw the need for and benefit of creating police departments

9. Railroad K9 Patrols

and hiring their own agents.[15] When railroading in North America experienced its peak during and immediately after World War II, the railroads employed approximately 9,000 railroad police officers in the United States and Canada. They served 400 different railroads and territory of 225,000 miles of track.[16] As passenger rail became the primary mode of transportation across the country in the mid–1940s, railroad police became responsible for the safety of passengers on and off the trains.

Police were often stationed in railroad stations and depots to guard against the nefarious activity of pickpockets, robbers, and those intent on mischief or criminal activity against the railroad passengers or crew. However, as the development of the interstate highway system in the 1950s resulted in more automobiles, rail travel diminished, and some downsizing of railroad employees, including the rail police, occurred. Technology and engineering also played a role in downsizing the railroad police forces, as more powerful locomotives made fewer stops and provided less opportunity for burglary at those points. Modern technology also provided an increased ability to secure freight.[17]

The railroad police's role has remained to protect the railroads' passengers and cargo from vandalism and theft and threats. The railroad police and special agents are usually paid by the railroad companies but have the same training and standards as other police officers, state or local, and the authority to conduct investigations and make arrests for crimes committed against the railroad. In some agencies, such as Amtrak, officers attend the Federal Law Enforcement Training Academy as part of their training.[18] Railroad police are fully sworn police officers. The extent of their jurisdiction varies from state to state. They can usually act as any other police officer in that state on law enforcement matters concerning the railroad. The railroad police use the latest technology to catch criminals, from night vision scopes to thermal images, and utilize special units to handle various situations, including their four-legged partners, the railroad K9 team.[19]

Dogs joined the railroad police force as special agents and emerged as valuable assets to assist the human police officers in patrolling the rails. Police dogs have a long history in law enforcement and police work. They protect handlers, engage in search and rescue, and identify explosives. German shepherd and Belgian Malinois are some of the most common breeds used for search roles.[20]

The first canine training program in the United States began in

Dogs of the Railways

New York. Word spread to the U.S. of the successful police K9 training program in Belgium. In 1907, Brigadier General Theodore A. Bingham, the New York police commissioner, sent Inspector George R. Wakefield to study the Belgian training program. Wakefield returned to the states with five Belgian sheepdogs, began a breeding program, and used the dogs for police work. By 1911, 16 dogs and handlers were trained. The new teams deployed out to residential areas on Long Island. The dogs ran loose in the neighborhoods from 11 p.m. to 7 a.m. They learned to chase and tackle anyone encountered during their shift, stand on their chests, and bark until their police officer handlers arrived.[21] But there were training problems. The training had not integrated social skills training for the canine recruits. The dogs the New York Police Department raised were given limited time with the public or civilians and were trained to respond only to law enforcement officers. Unless a person wore a police uniform, the dog was taught to view him or her as hostile. Dogs were trained to search houses and tackle perpetrators by wrapping their front paws around the target's lower legs and dragging them down.[22] These skills did not make for a community-friendly K9 officer, and complaints followed. By 1918, the K9 unit was disbanded.[23]

At the end of World War II, a renewed awareness grew of the benefit of using police dogs. After seeing the successful use of dogs during the war in England and by private organizations, American law enforcement began implementing K9 programs.[24] The early and mid–1950s saw a surge in K9 training programs; the dogs were trained to scale walls, enter a vehicle and hold its occupants, disarm a man, search buildings, and be vicious or gentle on command. Not all the programs were successful; even after purchasing five more German shepherds and six Doberman pinschers, the Portland Canine Corps was unsuccessful and disbanded.[25] Still, law enforcement had learned that a trained and loyal raildog could make a difference in keeping the railways safe. It was clear dogs were great partners for railway detective work.

When bloodhounds like Sheba's Bob (Chapter 4) began detective work for the Long Island Railroad, they set in motion a tradition of working dogs who protected the rails. When Superintendent Robert E. Kirkham of the Long Island Railroad police brought Sheba's Bob and the bloodhound recruits on the team, it started a rich history of using canine noses to track criminals and keep the railroad safe. Sheba's Bob and his team of floppy ears and noses to the ground were just the investigators for the job. The work of the bloodhound detectives resulted in a

9. Railroad K9 Patrols

drop in crime on the railroad, especially the dynamiting of station safes and thefts.

In 1956, the Baltimore City Police Department instituted the first modern canine corps in the United States. During the same time, the Los Angeles Police Department attempted to do the same and saw the many benefits of having a canine corps but had few areas that required foot patrols. Given the widespread use of motor vehicle patrols, the Los Angeles Police Department didn't see how the costs could outweigh the rewards. However, Baltimore's program was so successful that it garnered attention across the United States, prompting nearby police departments to request specialized training to create their own K9 units. After visiting the Baltimore training facility in 1959, the police department in Lancaster, Pennsylvania, had five volunteer handlers ready for service.[26]

Dogs are now a valuable part of the team that guards the rails of America. Law enforcement and safety are critical considerations for today's rail passengers. During the 1980s and early 1990s, transportation agencies developed canine programs in response to the need for improved security and emergency preparedness. K9 officers protected assets and functional areas of railroads.[27]

In 2002, the National Academies of Sciences, Engineering, and Medicine published a study on the role of canine officers in public transportation as a guide for decision-makers as they developed and implemented programs.[28] At the time of the study, 12 public transportation systems had K9 programs in operation: Bay Area Rapid Transit, Chicago Transit Authority, Massachusetts Bay Transportation Authority, Metropolitan Atlanta Rapid Transit Authority, Metropolitan Transportation Authority of Harris County, New York City Transit, New Jersey Transit, Niagara Frontier Transportation Authority, Port Authority Transit Hudson, Southeastern Pennsylvania Transportation Authority, Tri-County Rail, and Washington Metropolitan Area Transit Authority. The study authors interviewed more than 40 organizations that supported or deployed canine officers to determine the challenges and roles of implementing K9 programs.[29] The report then outlined the role of canine officers in many of the units and the various functions they performed to guard the railways. The roles included the following:[30]

- Serving as deterrent patrols in stations, platforms, transfer centers, and parking areas
- Supporting security for special events and crowd control
- Tracking persons

Dogs of the Railways

- Performing safety checks of transportation facilities
- Monitoring bridges, overpasses, and Amtrak stations for presidential visits
- Pursuing persons
- Defending or protecting safety officers
- Supporting narcotic searches
- Detecting explosives
- Protecting assets
- Assisting other police departments
- Protecting customer goods
- Patrolling train traffic

Training

Dogs who are potential guardians of the railways enter training early. The human officers are trained, too, and learn to recognize changes in their dog's behavior, which signals that the dog may have found something explosive. Humans and canine officers must be prepared to respond when the dogs' talents are needed.[31]

Caring for a police dog recruit is caring for a natural athlete, and handlers must ensure the canine partner gets proper exercise and nutrition and help to stay fit. Police dogs need affection, love, and playtime like any companion dog when they are not on the clock, and handlers spend time building the bond through off-duty playtime, off-duty outings, integration work, and exercise. The U.S. Police Canine Association Foundation provides education, training, and certification in the careful handling and training of police canines and other working dogs to advance public safety.[32] Certification usually covers obedience, agility, evidence, and suspect search. Training includes acclimating the dogs to a transportation environment since dogs can have a range of reactions to trains.[33] Typical training might consist of the dogs riding in train cars and getting used to the train's motion, which might feel different to the dog.[34] They get to practice walking through a train filled with passengers.[35]

The Transportation Security Administration (TSA) National Explosives Detection Canine Program trains and deploys canine teams who operate in mass transit and other environments. The training facility is located at Joint Base San Antonio-Lackland in San Antonio. It includes indoor and outdoor venues, including a cargo facility, a baggage claim area, a light rail station, a light rail car, two mock terminal parking lots, and the interior of an aircraft with open area search venues.[36] TSA canine teams are deployed nationwide. They screen passengers and cargo and support security. Many of these are assigned to rail facilities. The TSA reports that the teams logged over 300,000 duty hours throughout the country. They work at more than 100 of the nation's airports and mass transit and maritime systems. A variety of breeds are utilized in the program: German shepherds, Labrador retrievers, German shorthaired pointers, wirehaired pointers, vizslas, Belgian Malinois, and golden retrievers.[37] The dogs are used in most of the handlers' duty time. Recruits train at the San Antonio area airport, AT&T Center, and bus terminal.[38]

Regardless of the tracks and stations they patrol, hard-working raildogs join a community of canine teams across America's railroads who partner with human officers to keep America's railways safe and secure.

The Guardians of the Railways

Amtrak

In 2019, Summer, a 9-year-old Labrador retriever, was honored with the 20th annual American Kennel Club Humane Fund ACE Award for Canine Excellence. The award celebrates hard-working dogs who significantly improve the lives of their owners and communities. In the Uniformed Service K9 category, Summer was recognized for her role as a canine officer in the TSA as an explosive detection dog with the Amtrak Police Department in Washington, D.C.[39] Summer joined a new generation of raildogs who serve as guardians of the railways as canine officers with their human partners.

Summer began her career in the military and deployed to Afghanistan in 2012, where her duty involved sweeping and clearing areas for troops and searching for and identifying explosives. Summer retired from military service, met her new partner, and began training to certify as an explosive detection dog. With her partner, Sgt. Micah Jones, she completed training, including open-air training. Summer and Jones recertified yearly in a three-day process conducted by the TSA evaluators and a Lackland Air Force trainer. They worked a 10- to 12-hour day, and the return ride home gave the team some time to unwind.[40]

Dogs of the Railways

Summer and handler Jones dedicated their lives to protecting their community.[41] These working partners have a special bond.[42]

A team of canine officers with mini badges attached to their collars often greet the onboarding public on Amtrak trains.[43] The raildogs are on duty to serve as the first line of defense for explosive detection. It's a big job. Over 650,000 people go through Penn Station daily, more than the number traveling through all three New York City–area airports combined.[44]

The Amtrak Police Department K9 teams provide a physical and operational deterrent to potential threats from explosives. The teams deploy at stations throughout the system and conduct train rides and right-of-way patrols. They are part of an interagency initiative of the TSA, the federal and state departments of Homeland Security, and local and state governmental agencies. As of 2019, Amtrak reported it had the most K9 officers in the railroad industry with vapor wake capabilities, where they train to alert on passing individuals.[45] Humans and dogs often work 10-hour shifts.

The Amtrak K9 officers can be seen hard at work on patrol through New York's Penn Station. The dogs have to be people-friendly, but there is a "look but don't touch" policy, although taking a photo with the dog is allowed. The K9 unit at Amtrak works out of the Special Operations unit and is the first line of defense for explosives in the mass transit system.[46] The dogs work in a busy, urban environment.[47] They live with their human partner.

Keeping commuters safe at Penn Station is a big job for the raildogs. Over 10.4 million passengers take Amtrak through Penn Station each month.[48] Amtrak operates a nationwide rail network, serving more than 500 destinations in 46 states, the District of Columbia, and three Canadian provinces, on more than 21,400 miles of routes. During the fiscal year 2020, Amtrak customers took 16.8 million trips, a year-over-year decrease of 15.2 million passengers, because of pandemic-related travel demand reductions. On an average day, customers made nearly 46,200 trips on Amtrak trains.[49] The Amtrak rail system spans the country, and its national police force protects its customers, employees, and stakeholders.

Congress created Amtrak in 1970 to take over most of the intercity passenger rail services previously operated by private railroad companies in the United States. Amtrak is managed as a for-profit company rather than a public authority.[50] More than 400 sworn and civilian personnel at more than 30 locations in 46 states provide security measures

9. Railroad K9 Patrols

to keep the railways safe and secure. The Amtrak police perform traditional policing functions on the trains, at the stations and Amtrak facilities, and on the right of way. They also provide support for special events and significant weather events.[51]

The Amtrak canine officers are a vital part of the team, responsible for security for New York, New Jersey, and as far north as New Haven, Connecticut. Each unit undergoes an 11-week training program at Auburn University's canine detection program[52] or the canine center at Texas's Joint Base San Antonio-Lackland. In 2012, TSA opened its own training center.[53] Amtrak dogs are deployed at stations throughout the Amtrak system and provide physical and psychological deterrents to protect from potential threats.[54] The dogs pick up scents from humans and detect the specific scents that combine to make up an odor. They train to pick up scents "left in the wake" of a person. According to Captain Deborah Myers of the Amtrak K9 unit, the dogs "are more dependable than any piece of equipment."[55]

Bay Area Rapid Transit

Catch a ride on Bay Area Rapid Transit (BART), and you will likely see working raildogs and their two-legged partners walking through train cars, stations, and parking facilities. The dogs walk silently, looking around their beat. "He wants to work," explained BART Police K-9 Unit Officer Mike Zendejas of his partner, Tim a 95-pound German shepherd with big paws, alert eyes, and enormous energy.[56]

The BART began using canines for police work in the early 1970s, and the unit took different forms over the years. Since the terrorist acts of September 11, 2001, and subsequent bombings in subway systems from Madrid to Moscow, the dogs' role has expanded to another crucial area—detecting explosives, and BART Police Department canines are trained in explosives detection; K9 teams deter crime and terrorism through highly visible patrols and explosives-detection capability.

The work of the canine railway police and their partners is based on teamwork and affection. The canines partner with an officer-handler; when not on the job, the dogs are part of the officer's family. The transit system has called its dedicated and highly trained K9s "BART's best friends."[57] Like many large public transportation systems, BART has used patrol dogs for years as a visible deterrent to crime and to assist officers in responding to reports of crimes. "The presence of a dog is usually enough," said Sgt. Jason Ledford, BART's K9 unit supervisor and a former handler himself. "Most people don't want to challenge the dog. Ultimately, it keeps the person we're dealing with safer, and it keeps the handler safer because we're not involved in having to apprehend someone physically."[58]

The canine teams are on duty every day on different BART trains, on different lines, and at different times. The Bay Area Rapid Transit is a heavy-rail public transit system that connects the San Francisco Peninsula with East Bay and South Bay communities; its service extends to Millbrae, Richmond, Antioch, Dublin/Pleasanton, and Berryessa/North San José. It operates in five counties (San Francisco, San Mateo, Alameda, Contra Costa, and Santa Clara) with 131 miles of track and 50 stations, carrying approximately 405,000 trips on an average weekday (before the COVID-19 pandemic). The BART is a special purpose transit district formed in 1957 and opened for service in 1972. Its mission is to provide safe, reliable, clean, quality transit service.[59]

Houston METRO

The Metropolitan Transit Authority of Harris County (METRO) Police Department Canine Program assists with explosive detection throughout the Houston region. The canine program began in 1998 with a single narcotics canine. In the first few weeks, the program added explosive detection canines; several were cross-trained in patrol and tracking to assist with apprehending fleeing suspects. The METRO Police Department makes the teams' services available to many agencies across the Houston region—their police explosives-trained canines have assisted in searching for events such as the Major League Baseball All-Star Game, Houston Live Stock Show and Rodeo, Super Bowl, and National Basketball Association All-Star Game. The METRO K9 teams have won several National Narcotics Detector Dog Association's Regional Seminar competitions for explosives detection and patrol.[60]

Southeastern Pennsylvania Transportation Authority

The Southeastern Pennsylvania Transportation Authority (SEPTA) Police Department K9 units are assigned to high-risk stations that would typically require two officers. These teams are essential in detecting explosives and reducing felony crimes.[61] Created by

9. Railroad K9 Patrols

the Pennsylvania General Assembly, SEPTA is a large transit system, with fixed-route services, including bus, subway, light rail, trolleybus, Regional Rail, and ADA Paratransit and Shared Ride programs. This network assists Bucks, Chester, Delaware, Montgomery, and Philadelphia counties, with connections to New Jersey and Delaware.[62] In 2017, Jagger, a four-year-old German shepherd, worked in patrol and explosive detection. He patrolled the SEPTA system with his handler, Officer Jackie Trower. He lived with Trower and his family, including three children, their seven-year-old dog, and another shepherd. "Jagger has made himself at home with my kids and our other dog," said Trower. "He is not only my coworker; he is a member of my family."[63]

Burlington, Northern, and Santa Fe Railway

The Burlington, Northern, and Santa Fe (BNSF) Railroad K9 special agents ensure the security of the railroad. They patrol tracks, yards, and other rail facilities. High visibility of the K9 teams keeps the railroad secure. The BNSF K9 team training in narcotics detection, suspect apprehension, patrolling, and engagement standards is modeled after the National Police K9 Association.[64]

In 2019, Special Agent Nathan Allen and his K9 partner, Valet, worked at BNSF in Fort Worth, Texas. The police team of a human agent and K9 become true partners and train and live together to accomplish their role. "The interaction I have with my K9 partner offers a level of trust, understanding, and a relationship that is always evolving," said Allen. "The most rewarding part of being a K9 officer is that we can bring this trust and bond out to the field to support a more efficient and safer operation for us all."[65]

The K9 officer role on today's BNSF Railway covers a rail system that is the product of nearly 400 different railroad lines that merged or were acquired over 170 years. On February 12, 2010, BNSF became a subsidiary of Berkshire Hathaway, Inc. The BNSF averages 1200 trains rolling a day.[66]

Patrol dogs are treated as members of the workforce and the family. Each dog lives with the agent's family. However, they aren't household pets. Strict protocols must be followed by the officer when caring for the dog. "We want our K9s to be in a home environment that's protected and where they are cared for properly," explained

Dogs of the Railways

Luis Mares, deputy chief of resource protection. "But, we need to make sure that the household understands that the K9 is not a family pet or a toy, and they're willing to abide by our rules with having the K9 in the home."[67] The BNSF's police department primarily uses German shepherds, but sometimes other shepherd-like dogs join the force.

Port Authority

The Port Authority Police Department K9 Unit was formed in 1984. The unit consists of police officers and canine partners specializing in explosive or narcotics detection. The K9 teams work 24 hours a day, seven days a week, in all Port Authority facilities. The police officers and canines receive federal training at the Joint Base San Antonio-Lackland or through the Port Authority's K9 Training Unit, which has trained dogs for more than 40 outside agencies. The Port Authority Police K9 Unit's duties have included security for presidential, dignitary, and papal visits, as well as the United Nations General Assembly, Drug Enforcement Agency task force operations, K9 sweeps during the execution of state and federal search warrants, and K9 sweeps of all Port Authority facilities during periods of a high terror threat.[68]

New Jersey Transit Police K9 Unit

The New Jersey Transit Police Canine Unit is attached to its Special Operations Division. The K9 teams specialize in explosive and narcotic detection and criminal and missing person tracking searches throughout the New Jersey Transit system. On top of the hundreds of service calls handled each month and daily deployments, the police K9s assist municipal, state, county, and federal agencies with K9-specific operations. Each K9 team goes through an initial state certification process that ensures that they are competent in their abilities.[69]

Bonding and Belonging

The bond of the K9 officer with the handler is the driving force that propels the four-legged officer to serve with such distinction. The K9

9. Railroad K9 Patrols

New Jersey Transit Police K-9 and Lieutenant, 2018, New Jersey Transit Police (Wikimedia).

officer rides the rails as a working dog and finds a home in the officer's heart at the other end of the leash.

The bond between K9 officers and their human partners begins the day they meet. This bond is essential to the team's work and dedication.[70] Don Slavik wrote canine training articles for the United States Police Canine Association on building a bond with the canine partner. Slavik described "lots of training, lot of long nights, a lot of care required, and lots of love."[71] Police dogs live with their partners, so it's a 24/7 responsibility. Long nights are part of the job because many missions occur in the middle of the night. At night or after a shift, the canine guardians of the railway go home to a railroad family.

Raildogs, like humans, search for a path to find both love and belonging. Humans and dogs are social creatures. We both need affection and a sense of purpose. The role of the canine guardians of the railway is a testament to the railway dog's mission: to love and work. When the working raildogs created a canine presence on America's rails, they paved the way for a new generation of companion dogs to gain access and be welcomed on America's passenger trains.

10

Companion Pets Hop on Board, 2015 and Beyond

For decades, companion dogs were not allowed on passenger trains. But access to today's passenger trains changed for rail-riding pooches. Dogs like Brownie, Shep, and Roxey had settled for whatever comfort measures and kindnesses their adopted railroad family extended. Today, a companion dog no longer has to steal his or her way onto the railroad or be carried as freight—passenger railroads increasingly welcome companion dogs on board. Fluffy and Rover ride America's passenger trains with their human family.

* * *

Access to passenger train travel for companion dogs changed in 2015, due in part to then–Representative Jeff Dunham, Republican of California. Rep. Denham credited Lily, his 15-pound French bulldog, as his inspiration. Lily frequently traveled with the Denham family to and from California, and Denham questioned why he could take her with him on a plane but not a train.[1] Lily once was rejected by Amtrak to travel as a passenger with Denham en route. With three cosponsors, Denham sponsored a House bill, the Pets on Trains Act, HR2066, to let passengers board trains with their companion dogs and cats.[2] The bill provided a pilot program for Amtrak to designate at least one car per train, where feasible, for pets so that passengers "may transport a domesticated cat or dog in the same manner as carry-on baggage."[3] When the bill was introduced, the Humane Society supported legislation allowing pets to be brought on Amtrak.[4] Although the bill did not become law, it did provide the impetus for a pilot project for companion pets on Amtrak.

In May 2014, Amtrak and the Illinois Department of Transportation collaborated on a 6-month pilot program for companion pets on trains. Amtrak travelers were allowed to bring their small cats or dogs on trains between Chicago and Quincy.[5] An estimated 20 small animals had already been safely transported since April 2014 between Chicago and Quincy on these two trains. The pilot program was initially scheduled to end in November. Amtrak and Illinois gave the concept an extended trial through April 26, 2015. They expanded the project to a second downstate route. The pilot project allowed travelers to bring their pets on trips to and from Chicago and downstate Illinois. Dogs or cats up to 20 pounds were accepted in carriers such as those used in airplane cabins and placed under the seat of each pet guardian. Amtrak routinely welcomed service animals on trains at no charge, and that policy did not change.

Support grew for the project. Representative Denham pointed out the value of the Pets on Trains pilot, "The expansion of the Pets on Trains pilot program is a step forward in allowing families nationwide to travel with their pets on Amtrak trains. I look forward to continuing to work with Amtrak to see the program succeed." Acting Illinois Transportation Secretary Erica Borggren added, "Accommodating pets on trains is just one more way that Amtrak is an increasingly attractive option for travel in Illinois."[6] By 2016, the successful Amtrak Pets on Trains program grew to include most long-distance and state-supported trains, allowing customers to travel with their pet in a carrier for trips of up to seven hours.[7] Today Amtrak continues to support accommodating pets on the train, and most U.S. railroads have established policies for travel with companion pets.

Other events worked to open access to pets on trains. Transport regulations on other pets became more flexible after Hurricane Katrina, when it was discovered that some people refused the mandatory evacuation through public transport because their animals couldn't accompany them.

Companion Dogs Onboard

Access to rail service has expanded travel opportunities for dogs. Today rail systems have varying policies for companion animal riders, and policies vary by the rail carrier. Most policies specify the types and size of pet carriers, have rules related to the health and behavior of dogs riding the train, and require that they not be a nuisance to other passengers and be on a leash or harness at all times. Some require proof of vaccination and release of liability paperwork to be signed before travel. Most have weight limits or carrier size requirements that limit the size

10. Companion Pets Hop on Board, 2015 and Beyond

of the pets able to travel. Policies evolve and change, so up-to-date travel planning with a dog is critical to companion pets' travel success. Policies on companion dogs do not cover service dogs since service dog access is ensured under the Americans with Disabilities Act. Service dogs are those who assist a person with a disability, while therapy dogs are considered companion dogs for train travel.

The following are some rail systems that account for large numbers of rail services throughout the United States and welcome companion pets on board.

Amtrak

As the National Railroad Passenger Corporation, Amtrak provides medium- and long-distance passenger rail service, with 21,000 route miles in 46 states, the District of Columbia, and three Canadian provinces, and operates more than 300 trains each day to more than 500 destinations.[8] Dogs are now welcome on most routes. Amtrak welcomes pets onboard nearly all its trains with several guidelines.[9] Amtrak does not ship pets or allow them to travel as checked baggage; a companion dog must travel with a human.[10] Cats and dogs at least eight weeks old and weighing twenty pounds or less are allowed. A total of five pets are allowed per train, one per customer, and pet reservations are made on a first-come, first-served basis. Service animals do not count toward this limit. A pet fee is required for each leg of travel. Pets may travel in coach class but are not allowed in food service cars and other areas such as sleeping cars or business class. Some Amtrak routes designate a specific car for pets, and some routes allow pets and riders to travel on any coach car. Total travel time for companion pets is limited to seven hours, including transfer times.

Pet guardians must provide a pet carrier, which may be hard- or soft-sided but must be leak proof and well-ventilated. The pet carrier counts as one piece of carry-on baggage. The maximum weight of twenty pounds includes the pet with the carrier. The maximum size for pet carriers is 19" long × 14" wide × 10.5" high, and the pet must be able to sit, lie down, and remain entirely inside without touching the sides of the carrier. Pets must stay in their carrier while on board the train and at the station, must be with their human handler at all times, and may not be left alone while traveling. On most Amtrak trains, the traveler must place the pet carrier under the handler's seat, not the seat in front of the handler.

The handler must certify that the dog is current on all vaccinations and sign a pet release and indemnification agreement for each leg of travel at check-in.[11] Travelers must check in at the ticket office no later than 30 minutes before departure to take care of the confirmation. At unstaffed stations, the conductor confirms pet eligibility and provides documents for signature. Some restrictions apply on some Amtrak routes: Acela Express allows pets on weekends and holidays only, and travel with pets is not available on the Adirondack, Maple Leaf, and Amtrak Cascades in Canada and not available on Auto Train, Keystone Service, San Joaquins, Capitol Corridor Pacific Surfliner, or Thruway Connecting Services.

Additional and updated Amtrak pet carrier specifications are listed on the Amtrak policy on the website.[12]

California Transportation Systems

The requirements of the California transportation system for companion pets on board vary. Emotional support, therapy, comfort, and companion animals are welcome aboard the Los Angeles County Metropolitan Transportation Association (Metro). Pets must be secured in enclosed carriers and cannot block the aisle or a doorway, deprive a customer of a seat, or interfere with the comfort or convenience of other customers. LA MetroLink, a commuter and regional rail system in Southern California, requires that any pet be fully enclosed in a pet carrier that fits either on the passenger's lap or under the passenger's seat. This option limits travel to small dogs in a compact pet carrier.

The Bay Area Rapid Transit System (BART) allows pets to be brought aboard at no additional charge and requires that the pet be secured in a container manufactured explicitly for transporting a pet. Dogs must be on a leash or a harness. Non-service animals must be fully contained inside an enclosed carrier that can be held on the human traveler's lap.[13] The San Francisco Municipal Railway (Muni) does not allow any pets on the train during peak hours.[14] Leashed and muzzled dogs can ride during off-peak hours but must pay a fare, and dogs have to sit on passengers' laps or under their seats.

Long Island Railroad

The Long Island Railroad (LIRR) has 124 stations and more than 700 miles of track, with the passenger railroad system totaling 319 miles of the route. Small domestic pets are permitted, provided they are carried in kennels or similar containers that can be accommodated on the passenger's lap and that the dog can travel without annoyance to other passengers.[15]

Dogs and other pets are now recognized as family, and the LIRR has extended its welcome to accommodate this new definition of family. An illustration of this relationship occurred with the LIRR rescue of Sampson, an 8-year-old English bulldog, who wandered away from his owner and onto some train tracks on the LRR. In March 2021, *The New York Post* reported that LIRR Engineer Christian Beck travelling on the 10:10 a.m. Montauk-bound LIRR train out of Jamaica scooped up the pup after spotting him hanging next to the tracks east of the Southampton station at around 12:10 p.m. Beck said the LIRR crew had "enough time to react and slow the train" to pick up Sampson. Beck and his rail coworkers brought Sampson onto the train, gave him water, and continued on their way to Montauk, arriving on time at 12:54 p.m. In Montauk, conductor Mike Stabile posted Sampson's photo onto LIRR worker Face book groups, asking colleagues to spread the word. Meanwhile, Sampson enjoyed the ride and settled in. The LIRR crew made contact about 20 minutes later with Sampson's owner, who saw the posting on the social media site after a coworker sent him a link. "He followed me around the whole day," the railroad man said. "When I was on the couch in the break room, he took a nap right in front of me. He just hung out."[16]

Chicago Transit Authority

The commuter rail system in the Chicago metropolitan area permits small pets in enclosed carriers on non–peak period weekday trains arriving in and departing Chicago during certain hours and on all weekend trains. However, there is no guarantee that pets can be accommodated in the event of overcrowding. Only small pets in carriers are allowed. Carriers are not allowed to take up seats or seating areas or obstruct pathways on trains or in stations and must be small enough to be carried on by a single person. Carriers must fit in a passenger's lap or under the seat. The system reserves the right to remove passengers with pets that are noisy or disturb other customers.

Subways, Buses, and Commuter Rail

A growing number of urban dogs also have access to rail transportation on public transit. Though restrictions exist, most cities allow certain pets to ride on the subways and buses.[17] Each city has its own regulations regarding pets and public transit. Dog travelers on the New York Metropolitan Transportation Authority (MTA) must be in a carrier and not be a nuisance to other riders. There's no limitation on the container size.[18] Washington, DC's Metro allows pets in carriers they cannot escape.[19] Only small pets in carriers are allowed in Chicago, and the carrier cannot take up a seat or block pathways.[20]

Service dogs do not have the same restrictions as companion pets. Service dogs are not the same as therapy dogs or those used for emotional support.[21] A list of pet policies on the U.S. railroad is available from Woof Advisor and other travel sources[22]

Raildog Good Citizenship

With new privileges come new responsibilities, and today's traveling raildogs must be good rail citizens. Companion dogs must be healthy, well groomed, and up-to-date on vaccines. A canine rail traveler must be socialized to deal with busy transit locations' sights,

A companion dog and his human companion enjoy a ride on a train, 2017 (Wikimedia).

10. Companion Pets Hop on Board, 2015 and Beyond

sounds, and smells. The raildog's human travel companion should be diligent in checking railroad-specific requirements, carrying required paperwork, and keeping their dog on a leash. Sticking to nonpeak travel hours can make the rail journey more accessible and allow quality time to enjoy human-animal bonding and the romanticism of a train journey together.[23] Not all fellow rail travelers are dog fans, so the raildog should not be allowed to approach other travelers uninvited.

Today raildogs are welcomed as family members on many American passenger trains. They ride as precious family members and enjoy the sights, sounds, and adventures of train travel alongside their favorite humans. Their welcome on the rails was paved by the raildogs gone before who established treasured relationships with the railroad communities of America.

11

International Raildogs, 1953–2016

American dogs weren't the only canines hopping on trains or taking up residence in railway stations. Trains and railroads worldwide attracted enterprising pooches intent on an adventure or searching for home and family. The British dogs like Railroad Jack of Lewes station in England and the British collecting dogs (Chapter 2) became celebrities, but the Brits and Americans weren't the only ones to boast famous raildogs. Dogs were part of the railroad story and members of railroad families across the globe. Railroads in Italy, Russia, and Japan were home to famous vagabond canines of the railways.

* * *

Lampo: The Traveling Dog of Italy

In 1953, a small white mongrel jumped off a train at a railway junction at Campiglia Marittima on the line between Pisa and Rome, where Elvio Barlettani was an assistant station master. Elvio noticed the friendly dog and let the stray sleep at the station. Sensing an opportunity for a new friend and meal ticket, the dog soon followed Elvio everywhere, including the restaurant where Elvio regularly had lunch. The first time Elvio discovered the dog trailing him, he gave the pup a bowl of soup. With that, Elvio and Lampo sealed their friendship agreement. Soon Elvio's entire family befriended the dog.

The rail crew became fond of the stray pup and named the canine traveler Lampo (lightning) because the small pup moved fast. Lampo turned out to be a natural as a railroad dog. He was sociable and soon became friends with everyone at the station. A train station is a noisy and often hectic place. But the sights, sounds, and smell of the bustling railroad did not frighten the small dog. Instead, Lampo seemed fascinated by the railroad activity as he watched the loading and unloading of the trains.

The station had many benefits for the formerly homeless pup. Lampo maintained close surveillance of the trains and his pals, the railway men. Eventually, the railmen even let Lampo ride on the locomotives. Lampo made it a habit to stand on the platform outside the dining car as the express trains rolled past him. One day Elvio followed him and saw Lampo go straight to the platform just as the Turin Xpress pulled in. Lampo scanned the Turin train windows when he got alongside the diner. Elvio saw the cook lean out the window and throw some bones covered with meat. From that day forward, the train cooks would throw Lampo some bones and treats as the locomotive passed. Lampo would arrive at the platform just as a transfer pulled in, regardless of what time they came.[1]

Lampo adopted the station and rail family as his home and began a daily routine. He began his morning with a trip by train from Campiglia Marittima to Piombino to accompany Elvio's daughter Mirna to school. He took another train home and kept the stationmaster company until it was time for Lampo to return on the noon train to pick Mirna up and Lampo and his young friend traveled home together.

Lampo became so adept at timekeeping that passengers relied on him to alert them for train arrivals. When Lampo ran out of the ticket office and to the platform, waiting passengers knew their express train was coming soon.

Lampo expanded his routes even further and became an experienced and savvy traveler. He traveled on trains visiting Rome, Leghorn, and Pisa. If Lampo headed for Florence, he changed trains at Pisa and reversed the process on his journey home. Once Lampo hopped on the southbound train to Rome but by mistake chose the fast north express, which had no stop at Campiglia Marittima. This mistake was only a temporary setback for the clever Lampo. He just changed trains at Pisa and picked a local train that dropped him back home at the Campiglia station. Elvio would see him casually getting off a freight or a fast passenger train as if nothing unusual had happened. Lampo soon learned to distinguish the slow trains from the fast ones and the different train cars. When the railway men hung a tag on Lampo that read "Free Pass for Lampo the Traveling Dog,"[2] Lampo could travel almost anywhere because the station personnel enjoyed watching him.

Dogs of the Railways

Lampo became famous. Stories of Lampo's excursions became widespread in newspapers and by word of mouth, and soon Lampo was a celebrity. People came to see Italy's traveling dog, and he received fan mail. Rail passengers looked for him when they traveled his routes. The Italian newspapers featured stories about him. How he developed his ability to navigate the trains and routes was a mystery. No one understood how he knew what train went where and when it came and went. Nobody knew how he managed to get on the right one to get back home. This mystery only added to Lampo's popularity and fame. His admiring public offered theories and humorous explanations as to how he managed to navigate his complicated journeys.[3] One was that maybe he could read train schedules; another was that he could recognize train numbers. Still, no one could explain how he left in one direction and returned in the opposite direction.

Not everyone was a fan of the traveling dog. A few people complained about Lampo traveling without a leash or muzzle. It didn't help that Lampo would growl at some travelers. After he got stuck in a carriage door and the train he was traveling on had to be stopped to free him, he lost his welcome on the train. When a new stationmaster was appointed at Campiglia Marittima who disapproved of the attention given to the traveling dog of Italy, he banished Lampo from the station, his adopted home. Poor Lampo was put on a long-distance cargo train to Naples against Elvio's objections. Undaunted, Lampo returned on the Rome Express two days later. The unhappy stationmaster was determined to rid the station of the annoying dog once and for all, and Lampo was sent away again, this time in the luggage-van kennel. Now no one knew where the beloved dog was. But Lampo wouldn't let anyone separate him from his railway family. Five months later, Lampo hopped off a Rome Express back home—but now, he was ill and frail. He had lost all his fur and was thin. It was clear Lampo had suffered hardship and had encountered significant challenges in finding his way home. Lampo's railroad family worried: How many trains had he had to hop before finding his way home?

The railway management gave up on banishing the beloved raildog, and Lampo became the permanent mascot for the train station. The railway family nursed their friend back to health. The stationmaster was replaced by a new stationmaster who was more humane and promised to keep Lampo as the traveling dog of Italy on the railroad for the rest of Lampo's days. Lampo resumed traveling, and his fame grew. The story of the dog traveling through Italy by train intrigued readers worldwide, and Lampo even received a king-size box of dog biscuits from an unknown fan from Buffalo, New York, by air mail. Newspapers referred to him as Lampo, the wonder dog of the railroad. In 1960, when Lampo was featured in the American magazine *This Week*, the publication devoted three pages to the traveling dog; Lampo's article was longer than an article in the same issue on John F. Kennedy.[4]

As Lampo aged, his health declined; he could no longer jump on or off trains at the Campiglio station and had to curtail his traveling. Elvio promised the aging Lampo that he would have a home with Elvio and his family for the rest of his days. He vowed to have Lampo buried under the Acacia tree near the station. By July 1961, Lampo's eyesight was failing. On July 22, 1961, he slipped under a train. The maneuvering cargo train in Campiglia hit the dog and killed him. The cargo train was off schedule, and Lampo, being the train timetable expert he was, did not expect it to be there. As Elvio had promised, Lampo was buried in the flowerbed at the foot of an acacia tree at the railway station. Lampo's obituary appeared in *The Daily Mirror* in March 1962.

Lampo was memorialized by the American publication *This Week* with a monument at the Campiglia Marittima railway station. The memorial still greets passengers and train workers today at the station. The monument portrays Lampo staring at the trains with a paw in the air, a stationmaster's hat and a signaling disc at his feet. Lampo became even more famous when Elvio Barlettani penned Lampo's biography, *Lampo the Traveling Dog*, in Italian. The biography was translated into English, French, and Japanese and had 15 editions through 2009.[5] This biography of Lampo is considered the leading source of information on Lampo and his career.[6]

Lampo's legacy is a symbol of independence and loyalty to his rail family, and the mystery endures of how he managed to go wherever he wanted.[7]

Russia: The Commuter Dogs of Moscow

Raildogs possess a unique ability to make the best of what the railroad environment has to offer. A group of urban Russian canine rail travelers is one of the best examples of this adaptability. These unique raildogs in Moscow learned how to adapt to street life in the busy city and navigate and thrive in the crowded complex caverns of the Moscow subways. Taking the Moscow subways was just one of many tactics

Dogs of the Railways

these strays developed to survive the urban wilderness and bitter winters. These raildogs didn't just hop on board; they seemed to know where they were going and even appeared to learn train schedules.

Stray dogs were not new to Moscow. Strays were mentioned by Russian writers as early as the late 19th century and dramatized by Chekhov in the short story "Kashtanka." It has been estimated that as many as 35,000 stray dogs made their home in Moscow at any given time.[8] Andrei Poyarkov of the A.N. Severtsov Institute of Ecology and Evolution, a biologist and wolf expert who has studied Moscow's dogs for over 30 years, estimated that the quantity of food available to stray dogs kept the total population of homeless dogs steady at between 35,000 and 50,000.[9]

Most of Moscow's commuter dogs were born homeless; others arrived on the streets as rejected or abandoned house pets. Poyarkov estimated that fewer than 3 percent of abandoned pet dogs live long enough to breed.[10] Of these, about 20 stray dogs took to riding the subways in Moscow and adapted their behavior to the traffic and life of the city.[11]

The streets of Moscow haven't always been friendly to homeless dogs. The number of strays became so great in the 1990s that they began to bite humans. At one time, metro employees attempted to keep the commuter dogs out of the subway,[12] but these efforts failed. Attempts to ban dogs on Moscow trains were not successful.

The attitude and strategy towards the street dogs later changed to affection and admiration. The raildogs won the hearts of Moscow commuters, and some human travelers even gave up their seats for weary canine travelers or helped provide shelter for the dogs for the frigid Moscow winter. The new approach was catching the dogs, neutering them, and providing food. The dogs, in turn, kept the city free of food, leftovers, and rats. The stray dogs of Moscow became known as Moscow's Metro Dogs or the Commuter Dogs of Moscow and became part of the Moscow rail system commuter family.

The Moscow dogs became savvy and amiable travelers. They learned to recognize and respond to human signals and adapt to changing environments. Dogs find positive reinforcement in treats and affection. Positive reinforcement for their behavior and the availability of food and emotional support attracted the homeless dogs to the subway. The Moscow raildogs foraged for food and greeted people.[13] According to one study, some dogs seemed to hop on board simply for entertainment and to see new places.[14] They had a knack for endearing themselves to their human travelers and using their charm to forage for food

11. International Raildogs, 1953–2016

and emotional attention. These raildogs rode the metro and understood the rules of traffic lights. They knew what trains to board, where to jump off, and how to identify someone likely to give them a treat. The dogs learned how to deal with the noise and activity of busy stations. Much like human commuters, they sometimes grabbed a quick nap on their trip. When this happened, a human passenger often just stepped around the sleeping dog.

Some dogs lived in the subway but didn't travel; others used the subway to travel short distances instead of by foot, and a third type took longer trips working the human crowd for treats and emotional tenderness. The more attention-seeking dogs tended to approach women carrying large shopping bags. The dogs learned to lie under seats without getting in the way of other passengers. The Moscow dogs became model commuters: they stood in line, were considerate of other passengers, didn't hog the seats, and never chatted loudly on phones.

Andrei Neuronov, a Russian expert on animal behavior, studied the Moscow commuter dogs and was interviewed by Sally McGrane for *The New Yorker* magazine in 2013.[15] Neuronov provided some history on how the street dogs became commuters. He explained that in the Soviet era, there were no dogs in the subway because the stray dog population was well controlled. Dogs started taking the train in Moscow after the Soviet collapse in the 1990s. When the Soviet-era controls faded, the dogs won their freedom to roam. The fall of the Soviet Union in the 1990s changed the structure of the Russian economy and the city's land-use patterns.[16] Many industrialists abandoned factories and moved their businesses to city centers. Large abandoned industrial complexes became an ideal shelter for stray dogs. However, that meant people (potentially carrying treats and tidbits) and food sources moved downtown. The hungry dogs followed.

With more wealth came more food and garbage and more opportunity for enterprising dogs. The homeless dogs learned to ride the subway because the urban environment offered the best chance for scavenging food. As Moscow's quality of life improved, there was more garbage and more scraps for dogs. The combination of more scraps of food to eat and less regulation encouraged the growth of the stray dog population, and they flourished, developing new and clever survival strategies along the way. Resourceful canines looked to the appealing environment of the railways. With the Russian winter, the dogs went underground into the tunnels winding into the train stations. They learned to navigate

Dogs of the Railways

the escalators and settled into the rail stations and the city's heart. Metro workers and train passengers fed them.[17] Animals can learn to use transport as a mobility tool rather than just a food source. Dogs, like humans, have learned to adapt to changing environments.

The Commuter Dogs of Moscow became skilled way finders in the complex Moscow transit system. But how did they do it? Biologists and animal behavior scientists like Andrei Neuronov have studied Moscow's commuter dogs for over 30 years to understand canine urban wayfinding and have developed some theories.[18] Some believe that the dogs use a combination of three information sources to find their way: utilizing the smells and sounds associated with each station, listening to how the stations are announced on the train, and keeping track of the time intervals between stops. One theory holds that they may be able to distinguish different stations based on scent. Some studies suggest that dogs often use many sensory cues to find their way and do not rely on smell alone.[19] Other possibilities are that lighting and specific passenger movement may help the metro dogs navigate the complex metro environment; some may even be able to remember the sound of the different railway stations, especially those associated with food. It has also been suggested that dogs can learn the names of the stations as they are called out and which ones are associated with food. Although we know that dogs can learn words, it's unclear whether they genuinely know the names of specific stations or associate some of them with food.[20]

What we know is that railroads are filled with repetitive activities. Peak rush hours, openings, and closings happen regularly in the transit system, encouraging the dogs' learning. Passenger movement predictability may also help dogs distinguish one station from another. Peak rush hour, openings and closings, and the nightly shutdown occur on schedule.[21] Just as the railroad runs on time, so did the Moscow commuter dogs.[22]

The street dogs of Moscow were memorialized with a statue called "Compassion," which sits in the Mendeleyevskaya metro station on the Serpukhovsko line in the Tverskoy District of Moscow. The statue commemorates the tragic story of Malchik, a black mongrel stray who lived there until 2002 when a fashion model stabbed the dog. She didn't like how Malchik barked at her terrier. The citizens of Moscow were outraged at the attack. A bronze monument was erected on the spot where Malchik met his sad end. Rail workers, commuters, and visitors now pass by and pat the bronze dog on his head for good luck, remembering

11. International Raildogs, 1953–2016

the story and the plight of the raildogs of Moscow who lived on the subways, stations, and streets.[23] Today as strays in Moscow have decreased, so have the number of commuter dogs seen on the subway.

Japan: Hachiko

Hachiko of Japan was one of the most famous international raildogs. For over two years, Hachiko would follow his guardian, a university professor, to the Shibuya train station, where the faithful dog would wait for his guardian's return from school. When Hachiko's beloved guardian died suddenly from a brain hemorrhage at work and never returned, Hachiko continued his daily vigil for ten years, waiting for his guardian to return to the station. Hachiko continued his watch until he died in 1935. The bronze statue stands where Hachiko stood vigil as a testament to loyalty and love. Hachiko's story provided the basis for the 2009 film *Hachi: A Dog's Tale*.

Campiglia Marittima train station: Statue for Lampo, the traveling dog (cf. Elvio Barlettani, 1962, Wikimedia).

Dogs of the Railways

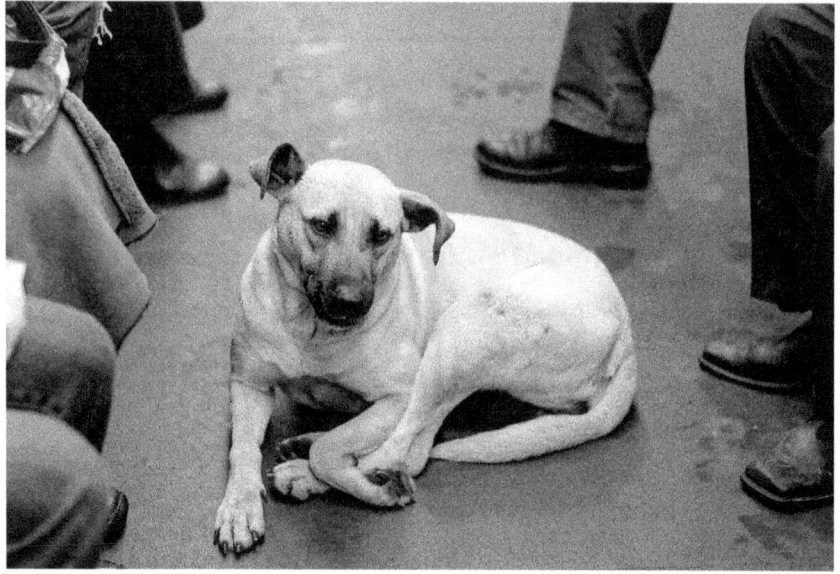

A Moscow Street Dog Riding the Subway, 2005 (Wikipedia).

These international raildogs navigated the railway world with skill and mysterious, uncanny abilities. Dogs across the world rode the rails and, in so doing, read human behavior and integrated themselves into the rhythm and routine of the railway and the railroad family lives. Both dogs and rail workers across the world were richer for their shared journey.

12

Raildogs

Finding the Way Home

Railroads changed American life and the raildogs were rock stars in the story of the American railroad. We have seen that a raildog often became as famous as the railroad. As trains were sources of romantic adventure and symbols of independence, the railroad dogs inspired equal admiration. An itinerant hard-luck dog or a loyal canine who kept a vigil on a train grieving for a beloved person charmed the hearts of America's railroad communities. A canine railway hobo or protector was irresistible. Along with the challenges of adjusting to changes brought by urbanization and industrialization, Americans were swept along with the excitement of the railroads, which were evolving from moving freight to being a comfortable and even luxurious means of transportation. Raildogs came along for the ride and the adventure.

Raildogs became famous in different ways. A raildog became a companion to a president and traveled on the commander-in-chief's funeral train, their last journey together, after Franklin D. Roosevelt died. Some raildogs mourned beloved humans or lost homes. Others found work and purpose on the rails, even pioneering new roles. As American communities faced and met each generation's challenges, the raildogs enriched their lives. They became charming actors and symbols of the unfolding drama of changing American life.

Dogs demonstrated powerful emotions to these communities: the power of grief and mourning, courage and bravery, and the human and animal need for belonging. Annie, a pregnant dog rescued by railroad men in the Great Depression, showed a community the enduring power of kindness even in hard times. The itinerant dogs became celebrities, mascots, hometown heroes, and media darlings. Railway dogs gave back to the communities that gave them their homes. They helped create community pride, spirit, philanthropy and policed rail communities.

They made people laugh when smiles were hard to come by—when danger and sadness were a way of life.

Raildogs changed the people who lived and worked in railroad communities and traveled the rails. Trains occupied an extraordinary place in the imagination. The lure of the open road, adventures, new beginnings, and their raildog lives conjured deep emotions in the American psyche. The railroad and depots were sites of romance, chance encounters, farewells, the meeting of strangers, and views of streams of faces disappearing in the crowd. The railroad attracted canine adventurers and human visionaries, dreamers, rogues, and drifters in an evolving America. In recent times, railroads and train stations present new dangers, and raildogs help travelers feel safe.

Four Themes

When these uncommon canines arrived in their railroad communities, they surprised the communities and people who met them. Most were ordinary dogs who lived an everyday life until they ventured from their familiar worlds and went into railroad life. Their human mentors often introduced animals into a new world of travel, and the raildogs stimulated a new vision of America or the railroad. Raildogs had great timing. Each dog pioneer wandered into the railroad life at his or her defining moment in the railroad's history, and when a charismatic dog trotted in, the pup was hard to ignore. Each, in his way, changed the railroad and the rail family.

The raildogs were a diverse collection of breeds and appearances. Raildogs ranged from obscure strays and scruffy wanderers to presidential pampered pooches, fearless detectives, and police officers. As diverse as the raildogs were in appearance and breed, could there be a common thread that defines a canine railroad hero? What common element did these dogs possess that caused them to adopt the railroad family as their own?

Their stories reveal four common themes: the human-animal bond; resilience; the search for a home, connection, and family; and finding the way home. These themes struck a chord for the human family who encountered them.

The Human-Animal Bond

The railway dogs show how the human-animal bond can exist today with an entire community. The stories of the raildogs are one of

12. Raildogs

the human-canine transformative connections that inspired communities during difficult times. The American Veterinary Medical Association defines the human-animal bond as "a mutually beneficial and dynamic relationship between people and other animals that is influenced by behaviors that are essential to the health and well-being of both."[1] As raildogs became objects of media attention and community devotion, the human-animal bond grew between dogs and an entire railroad community.

What about these raildogs could evoke a bond between a stray dog and an entire community? Stories of dogs who lived on the rails resonated with people seeking adventure and hope despite their often grim reality of daily life in a railroad community. The hardship narrative of the raildogs represented a vulnerability shared by the raildogs and the communities who adopted them. The loyalty of a dog who chose to stay with the railroad family, even after traveling wide and far, touched the hearts of communities long after the raildog's death.

Some dogs appeared to be riding the rails in hopes of reuniting with a beloved lost guardian. Humans often wondered if the dogs were mourning a loss and if rail-riding expressed the animal's grief. The vulnerability of an itinerant dog who appeared to be grieving for a lost guardian could evoke human emotions. This sense of shared vulnerability may have been responsible for the outpouring of affection and identification with the hard-luck canines of the rails. In her book *How Animals Grieve*, Barbara J. King, professor of anthropology at the College of William and Mary, explored mourning in animals. King suggested that as humans become aware that non-human animals love and grieve, knowing how much we share with other animals may be comforting.[2] Dogs that suffer and overcome hardship induce powerful emotions in humans.

Media coverage of the hardship or suffering of dogs has always evoked strong feelings in humans, sometimes overshadowing the adversity and distress of their human counterparts. In 2017, a team from Northeastern University in Boston and the University of Colorado at Boulder, writing in *Society and Animals*, studied whether people are more disturbed by dog or human suffering. They found more empathy for human children, puppies, and full-grown dogs under certain conditions than for adult human victims.[3] The study's conclusions might shed light on the power of the shared vulnerability of the dogs who rode the rails and the railroad communities that adopted them as their own.

Dogs of the Railways

Humans and non-human animals need to be connected. A human who yearns for adventure or a lost relationship can identify with a dog searching for interesting sights and locations or a lost love.

Resilience

The raildogs allowed their gifts to emerge as they showed, helped, and taught their human partners about resilience in challenging times by doing what they were best at—being dogs. They didn't just survive; they thrived—even in difficult circumstances. They adapted and found new homes and affection. The raildogs became symbols of the independent spirit of America. Dogs who rode the rails or lived within railroad communities represented independence of spirit, loyalty, and the search for home and life on one's own terms. The raildog detectives and guardians of the rails became sentries and warriors who helped their adopted communities feel safe during bad times and travels. Fala joined a nation in grief.

Their stories inspired Americans during challenging economic times, times of grief, and societal change. The hardship narrative of the raildogs represented a vulnerability shared by the dogs and the communities who adopted them. The loyalty of a dog who chose to stay with the railroad family, even after traveling far, touched the hearts of communities long after the raildog's death.

Some dogs appeared to be riding the rails or living in rail communities in hopes of reuniting with a beloved lost guardian. Humans often wondered if the dogs were mourning a loss and if rail-riding expressed the animal's grief. The vulnerability of an itinerant dog who appeared to be grieving for a lost guardian could elicit strong human emotions. This sense of shared vulnerability may have been responsible for the outpouring of affection and identification with the hard-luck canines of the rails. Dogs that suffered and overcame hardship evoked powerful emotions for humans.

Dogs of the railways searched for community, predictability, belonging, and a way home but defined on their own terms. The raildogs showed that family might not be an individual but a community. For these canine hoboes, the railroads became a welcoming fellowship of human and canine travelers taking a journey on their own terms.

The quests of the raildogs remind us of our own searches for home, love, belonging, and home. The stories of the raildogs show how this human-animal bond can exist today within a community and how the railroad became home to a remarkable group of canines.

12. Raildogs

The Search for Home, Connection, and Family

Dogs and people need to belong. We need to belong to a group or tribe.[4] Today, belonging to a group or family gives us a group identity and a sense of common purpose and support and helps us battle loneliness. Group identity has benefits. Belonging to a group and feeling identified with those in that group is essential to our identity and sense of self.[5]

In an increasingly technological world, dogs and other animals bring us the opportunity to connect—with our own species and with others. Animals and humans depend on each other. We occupy the same planet. In a world where we are all so connected, we have a mutual need and responsibility to care for each other and respect the unique gifts of each species. Today's guardians of the railways find home and purpose as police dogs guarding America's rail system. Their bond with their handlers and railroad family reminds us of how we connect with family—work family or other tribes that share a common purpose. Today, we see that our companion dogs are partners with us in the adventure of travel as passenger railroads across America welcome our pets on board.

The quests of the raildogs reveal our own searches for home, love, belonging, and the families we need and sometimes find. The people of the railroads bonded with itinerant railway dogs as both searched for belonging, community, adventure, safety, and constancy as the world around them changed. The raildogs loved trains, and the railroad community loved the dogs. The train and the railroad became a community—for an hour, a day, or a lifetime.

We began this book with a question. Why would a stray dog choose life on a train? Each raildog was propelled by his or her unique fate and circumstances.

Trains and railroad life attracted dogs to the tracks for many of the same reasons it attracted their human counterparts. Sometimes their job was on the railroad. For a dog, the railroad environment was appealing; trains felt good. There was an interesting clatter and a plentiful assortment of exciting whistles. The comings and goings of trains were predictable. For the most part, trains ran on schedule. Schedules matter to dogs. Life on a train and train stations occurs in small spaces, with changing landscapes and both familiar and unusual smells that appeal to dogs. Train journeys encouraged familiarity and casual camaraderie among human and canine travelers.

Dogs of the Railways

Communities often shun strays and view them as nuisances, pests, or dangerous canine thugs. Instead, the stray dogs of the railways became well-loved community dogs. Their home became the hearts of the people of the railroad. Many raildogs searched for community, predictability, belonging, and a way home, but with home defined on their terms. The raildogs showed that a family might not be an individual but a community. For these canine hoboes, guardians, companions, and philanthropists, the railroads became a welcoming fellowship of human and canine travelers taking a journey on their own terms. It's a search to which many humans can relate.

But the sad endings of some raildogs like Owney and Lampo and others are also a cautionary tale. Even raildogs get old and slow down. They don't always maintain their youthful vigor, charm, demeanor, and appearance. Not everyone understands that aging dogs might need special consideration and care. That might mean a less stressful setting than a busy railroad. Some railroad families perhaps did not understand the need to help an aging dog find a more comfortable, safe, and calm routine environment in which to spend his golden years.

Finding the Way Home

What can we learn from these dogs of the railways? The stories of the raildogs touched the human community; they stirred our imagination and emotions. A dog on a train could seem like a wistful traveler filled with dreams, motion and adventure, and often longing. We wonder: Where are they going and why? Some boarded trains in search of a beloved human or a home. Perhaps what intrigues us about the dogs who make the railroad their home is that we see them as common travelers on life's tumultuous journey.

These canine rail travelers became role models and heroic symbols as inspired humans shared the dogs' stories. Their stories became metaphors for the human railroad family. The raildog who searches for a lost guardian or adopts an entire railroad community as his family reminds us how we all long to feel connected to a community. Perhaps that explains why the people of the railways welcomed raildogs.

The stories of the raildogs intrigue us. We recognize the common yearnings of humans in our canine partners. Like dogs, we search for connections with human and animal friends. We yearn to be part of family and community. We need to work, love, and have a sense of purpose. We may be touched by stories of dogs who travel long distances

12. Raildogs

to reunite with a beloved human or their home. Homing abilities in dogs are not entirely understood. Researchers have found that dogs have several ways to navigate distances; in addition to following a scent trail back to their guardians or home, they may also employ a sort of canine navigation.[6] They are sort of "hard-wired" to do this; they use their canine ability to detect magnetic fields to navigate their environment. Dogs seem to have a unique ability to find their way home. Several hypotheses have been proposed, but this ability remains unexplained.[7]

Today, our modern companion dogs join us on board trains and make our rail journeys more enjoyable. With them by our sides, we understand a new definition of home: *home comes with us on our journeys when we travel with someone we love.* And perhaps, despite life's challenges, we are reminded by the raildogs that, somehow, we can always find our way home.

Appendix

Monuments and Memorials to Raildogs

The memory of famous raildogs lives on in memorials across the United States and the world:

Owney, Washington, D.C.

A figure of Owney is displayed at the National Postal Museum.

Roxey, Merrick Station, New York

At Merrick Station, Roxey is memorialized with a headstone donated by a group of female commuters in 1915. A water bowl built into the memorial is often filled with flowers.

Annie, Fort Collins, Colorado

Annie's headstone reads, "From the C&S Men to Annie Our Dog, 1934–1948," and a 2½-foot-tall statue of Annie stands in front of the town library and extends one paw to greet visitors. City officials considered moving the grave during the depot's renovation, but Annie's friends worked to get Annie's Mason Street gravesite listed as a historical landmark.

Shep, Fort Benton, Montana

A bronze sculpture by Bob Shriver, "Forever Faithful," honors Shep in Fort Benton.

Appendix

Fala, Washington, D.C.

Fala is honored with a statue in the F.D.R. Presidential Memorial.

Brownie, Victorville, California

A gravestone marks Brownie's final resting place at the Santa Fe Railroad Station in Victorville, California.

Chapter Notes

Introduction

1. Wolmar, *The Great Railroad Revolution*.

Chapter 1

1. "Owney Was Here."
2. Pope, "Braving the Rails"; Pope, "The Post Office's Best Friend."
3. Smithsonian National Postal Museum, "Owney the Dog"; Pope, "The Post Office's Best Friend."
4. Smithsonian National Postal Museum, "Owney the Dog"; Pope, "The Post Office's Best Friend."
5. "Owney Was Here."
6. Huggins, "Finding Railroad Jack."
7. "Owney Was Here."
8. Pope, "The Post Office's Best Friend"; *Los Angeles Times*, April 25, 1893.
9. *Boston Daily Globe*, December 13, 1894; Pope, "The Post Office's Best Friend."
10. Paine, "Owney's Travels."
11. "Owney, the Dog."
12. Cushing, *The Story of Our Post Office*, 84.
13. *Ibid*.
14. U.S. Postal Service, *The United States Postal Service: An American History*, 20.
15. Hingston, "11 Things You Might Not Know"; Betz, "The Postal Dog."
16. Smithsonian National Postal Museum, "Owney the Dog."
17. Bessette, "Owney the Postal Dog Rides Again"; Pope, "The Post Office's Best Friend."
18. "Owney's Travels."
19. Pope, "The Post Office's Best Friend."
20. Wales, *A Lucky Dog*.
21. Blitz, "Owney the Mail Dog Still Lives, Sort of, in DC."
22. "Rail by Mail: Needing a Good Luck Charm."
23. Pope, "The Post Office's Best Friend."
24. Smithsonian National Postal Museum, "The Creation."
25. *Ibid*.
26. Pope, "The Post Office's Best Friend."
27. Smithsonian National Postal Museum, "Expansion and Turmoil."
28. *Ibid.*; Smithsonian National Postal Museum, "A Day in the Life."
29. Smithsonian National Postal Museum, "Story of Owney."
30. *Ibid*.
31. Beauchemin, "Oral Histories B."
32. *Ibid*.
33. *Ibid*.
34. *Ibid*.
35. Toledo *Daily Blade*, June 12, 1897.
36. Pope, "The Post Office's Best Friend."
37. "The Dog Owney Dead at Last"; Roadside America, "Owney."
38. Toledo *Daily Blade*, June 12, 1897.
39. Smithsonian National Postal Museum, "Owney the Dog."
40. Smithsonian National Postal Museum, "Owney Silver Spoon."
41. Facebook, "Owney the Railway Mail Dog," https://www.facebook.com/owney/.
42. Smithsonian National Postal Museum, "Decades of Change."

43. *Ibid.*
44. Smithsonian National Postal Museum, "The Final Run."

Chapter 2

1. Bondeson, *Amazing Dogs*, 92–93. Bondeson's book is rich with the history and facts of a collection of amazing dogs and provided valuable source material and information about the railroad and Railway Jacks and the collecting dogs for this book.
2. "Railroad Jack Dead."
3. *Ibid.*
4. "Railroad Jack Is Dead."
5. "Railroad Jack on a Tour to the Pacific Coast."
6. "He Was a Baggage Car Dog."
7. "Railroad Jack Stolen."
8. "Railroad Jack Kidnapped."
9. "Railroad Jack Stolen."
10. "Albany's Columbus Day Celebration."
11. "He Was a Baggage Car Dog."
12. *Ibid.*
13. *Ibid.*
14. *Ibid.*
15. Kelli Huggins, a historian and museum professional, reports on her website that she is searching for facts about the final destination of Railraod Jack and preparing a book about him. See kellihuggins.com.
16. "Second Railroad Jack Killed."
17. Northwestern Pacific Railroad Historical Society, "NWP Railroad History."
18. Curious Wanderer, "Boomer Jacks."
19. Martin, "Somewhere Down the Line"; Phillips, "Boomer Jack."
20. Aubrey-Herzog, "Battle for Boomer Jack."
21. Gordon, "Railway Jack."
22. *Ibid.*
23. Bondeson, *Amazing Dogs*, 87.
24. Gordon, "Railway Jack."
25. *Ibid.*
26. Bondeson, *Amazing Dogs*, 89.
27. *Ibid.*, 90.
28. "Railway Jack."
29. Bondeson, *Amazing Dogs*, 111.
30. Bluebell Railway Museum, "London Jack."
31. Parkinson, "The Dead Dog That Changed Color Twice."
32. Bluebell Railway Museum, "London Jack."
33. Parkinson, "The Dead Dog That Changed Color Twice."
34. *Ibid.*
35. *Ibid.*
36. *Ibid.*
37. *Ibid.*
38. Bondeson, *Amazing Dogs*, 103.

Chapter 3

1. Gavan, "1904: Roxey the Long Island Railroad Dog."
2. *Ibid.*
3. Ziel and Foster, *Steel Rails to the Sunrise*, 205.
4. Worthington, *Miles of Smiles*.
5. "How Roxey Became a Long Island Pet."
6. Ziel and Foster, *Steel Rails to the Sunrise*, 205.
7. Sources spell Roxey's name both Roxey and Roxy. This chapter adopts the Roxey spelling.
8. Gavan, "1904: Roxey the Long Island Railroad Dog."
9. "How Roxey Became a Long Island Pet."
10. *Ibid.*
11. "A Dog with Many Masters."
12. *Ibid.*
13. Gavan, "1904: Roxey the Long Island Railroad Dog."
14. *Ibid.*
15. "A Dog with Many Masters."
16. *Ibid.*
17. Gavan, "1904: Roxey the Long Island Railroad Dog."
18. Ziel and Foster, *Steel Rails to the Sunrise*, 8.
19. *Ibid.*, 120–121.
20. Kalmbach, *The Historical Guide*, 174.
21. *Ibid.*
22. *Ibid.*
23. Middleton, *Manhattan Gateway*, 7, 96.
24. Kalmbach, *The Historical Guide*.

Notes—Chapters 4 and 5

25. *Ibid.*
26. PBS, *The Rise and Fall of Penn Station.*
27. *Ibid.*
28. Middleton, *Manhattan Gateway,* 7.
29. *Ibid.,* 97.
30. Ziel and Foster, *Steel Rails to the Sunrise,* 195.
31. *Ibid.*
32. PBS, *The Rise and Fall of Penn Station.*
33. Ziel and Foster, *Steel Rails to the Sunrise,* 203.
34. *Ibid.,* 172.
35. *Ibid.,* 24, 172.
36. "A Dog with Many Masters."
37. *Ibid.*
38. "How Roxey Became a Long Island Pet."
39. "Roxey's Appeal."
40. *Ibid.*
41. "The Passing of Roxey."
42. *Ibid.*
43. *Ibid.*
44. *Nassau Daily Review-Star,* June 10, 1939, page 9.
45. Ziel and Foster, *Steel Rails to the Sunrise.*
46. Roadside America, "Roadside Grave of Roxey the Railroad Dog."
47. Worthington, *Miles of Smiles.*
48. Williams, "The LIRR's Best Friend."

Chapter 4

1. "Dog a Real Sherlock Holmes."
2. *Ibid.*
3. *Ibid.*
4. "The Greatest of Dog Detectives."
5. Wolmar, *The Great Railroad Revolution,* 202–05, 215–09.
6. The Railroad Police, "History."
7. *The Garda Post* "Early Days of Railroad Policing to Present" https://garda-post.com/early-days-of-railroad-policing-to-present/.
8. "LIRR Thieves Caught with Bloodhounds' Aid."
9. Gavan, "The Dog Detectives."
10. Ruddell and Decker, "Train Robbery."
11. In 1989, railroad police were given interstate authority under U.S. Code 49: 28101.
12. "LIRR Thieves Caught with Bloodhounds' Aid."
13. "Police Department."
14. Gavan, "The Dog Detectives."
15. American Kennel Club, "Bloodhound."
16. "LIRR Thieves Caught with Bloodhounds' Aid."
17. "The Greatest of Dog Detectives"; The Railroad Police, "History"; MTA, "Only Mass Transit Oriented Police Canine Training Facility."
18. "LIRR Thieves Caught with Bloodhounds' Aid."
19. *Ibid.*
20. The Railroad Police, "History."
21. MTA, "MTA Police Department Opens Premier Canine Training Center."
22. *Ibid.*

Chapter 5

1. "Depot Dog's Memory Lives."
2. Fort Collins History Connection, "Annie the Railroad Dog."
3. *Ibid.*
4. *Ibid.*
5. Watrous, *The History of Larimer County.*
6. *Ibid.*
7. Werner, "Colorado and Southern Railway."
8. Kalmbach, *The Historical Guide,* 107–08.
9. "Colorado and Southern Freight Depot."
10. *Ibid.*
11. "Depot Dog's Memory Lives."
12. Fort Collins History Connection, "Annie the Railroad Dog."
13. Ahlbrandt, *Annie, The Railroad Dog.*
14. City of Fort Collins, "Operation Services."
15. Lang, "Dog's Gravestone Has Nine Lives."
16. Fort Collins Museum of Discovery, "Daily Discovery: Annie the Railroad Dog."
17. "Depot Dog's Memory Lives."

18. Humane Education Coalition, Website.
19. Gibbons, "Fort Collins Library Ends 'Annie Walk.'"
20. Coloradoan Staff, "10 Events That Shaped Fort Collins History."

Chapter 6

1. Several sheepherders are known to have died in 1936, but the identity of Shep's beloved guardian remains a mystery.
2. Montana Kids, "The Story of Shep"; Coppinger and Coppinger, "Dogs for Herding and Guarding Livestock."
3. Stover, *American Railroads*, 29.
4. *Ibid.*, 76.
5. River and Plains Society, *Man's Best Friend*.
6. Wolmar, *The Great Railroad Revolution*.
7. Robinson, "Shep Eternal: The Magical Life and Afterlife of Our World Famous Faithful Dog."
8. River and Plains Society, *Man's Best Friend*.

Chapter 7

1. Aronson, "Presidential Passage," 1.
2. Klara, *FDR's Funeral Train*, 97.
3. *Ibid.*, 232.
4. Hatch, *Franklin D. Roosevelt*, 374.
5. Bishop, *FDR's Last Year*, 623.
6. Franklin D. Roosevelt Presidential Library and Museum; Klara, *FDR's Funeral Train*, 9.
7. Bishop, *FDR's Last Year*, 623.
8. Kinsolving, *The Dogs of War*, 61–79.
9. *Ibid.*
10. American Kennel Club, "Scottish Terriers."
11. Suckley and Dalgliesh, *True Story of Fala*, 28.
12. Presidential Pet Museum, "FDR's Famous Scottish Terrier."
13. Suckley and Dalgliesh, *True Story of Fala*, 28.
14. *Atlanta* Magazine, "FDR: The Long Goodbye."
15. Kinsolving, *The Dogs of War*, 103.
16. History.com, "FDR Defends His Dog."
17. Jones, "The True Story of the Coolest Dog."
18. *Ibid.*
19. Tully, *FDR: My Boss*, location 2171–207.
20. National Archives, "Forward with Roosevelt."
21. Goodwin, *No Ordinary Time*, 548.
22. Llewellyn, "Paws, Pathos, and Presidential Persuasion."
23. Lindeblade, "Roosevelt Funeral Train."
24. Aronson, "Presidential Passage," 2.
25. Suckley and Dalgliesh, *True Story of Fala*, 421.
26. *Ibid.*
27. Aronson, "Presidential Passage," 1.
28. *Ibid.*
29. Carter, "Ferdinand Magellan Presidential Railcar."
30. Aronson, "Presidential Passage," 2.
31. Lengel, "Franklin D. Roosevelt's Train Ferdinand Magellan."
32. Carter, "Ferdinand Magellan Presidential Railcar."
33. Hassett, *Off the Record*, 146.
34. Suckley, *Closest Companion*, 189.
35. Klara, *FDR's Funeral Train*, 78; Monroe, "President's Special," 19.
36. Klara, *FDR's Funeral Train*, 131.
37. Aronson, "Presidential Passage"; *Atlanta* Magazine, "FDR: The Long Goodbye."
38. Tully, *FDR: My Boss*, location 6100–106.
39. *Atlanta* Magazine, "FDR: The Long Goodbye."
40. Kluckhohn, "Crowds in Tears."
41. Goodwin, *No Ordinary Time*, 215–16.
42. Roosevelt, *Autobiography*.
43. Kinsolving, *The Dogs of War*, 147.
44. Roosevelt, *On My Own*, 19.
45. Presidential Pet Museum, "FDR's Famous Scottish Terrier."
46. "Fala Buried in Hyde Park Garden."
47. National Park Service, "Fala."
48. Zimmerman, "The Who's Who of Grand Central."
49. *Ibid.*

50. Young, "Secret 'FDR Train Car.'"
51. Zimmerman, "The Who's Who of Grand Central," 68.
52. Schlichting, *Grand Central Terminal*; Zimmerman, "The Who's Who of Grand Central," 68.
53. Middleton, *Grand Central*; Zimmerman, "The Who's Who of Grand Central," 68.
54. Zimmerman, "The Who's Who of Grand Central," 68–69.
55. Young, "Secret 'FDR Train Car.'"
56. Ahmed, "A Grand Central Ghost Story."
57. "Pagan Beliefs Persist."
58. Herzog, "Encounters with Dead Pets"; Broadway, "Poll Finds America."
59. Llewellyn, "Paws, Pathos, and Presidential Persuasion."

Chapter 8

1. Route 66 California State Railroad Museum, "Brownie the Railroad Dog."
2. California State Railroad Museum.
3. Route 66 California Railroad Museum, "Brownie the Railroad Dog."
4. Moon, "Gravestone Stands as Tribute."
5. Warnick, "Dog's Grave Marker."
6. *Ibid.*
7. Great American Stations, "Victorville, CA."
8. *Ibid.*
9. Route 66 California Railroad Museum.
10. Waymarking.com, "Brownie the Railroad Dog"; Route 66 California Railroad Museum, "Brownie the Railroad Dog"; Cabe, "This Desert Life."
11. *Ibid.*
12. Steinbeck, *The Grapes of Wrath*, 118.
13. Victorville, "About Victorville."
14. National Historic Route 66 Federation, "Route 66 History."
15. Tuolumne County Historical Society, "Railroad Transportation."
16. *Ibid.*
17. Visit Tuolumne County, "Tuolumne County Facts."
18. Railtown staff, "Buster and Hobo."
19. *Ibid.*

Chapter 9

1. The Animal Medical Center is a large nonprofit animal hospital. Founded in 1910 as a temporary clinic to help animals whose owners could not afford medical care, AMC has more than 120 veterinarians working collaboratively across more than 20 specialties and services. The hospital maintains a level-one trauma center in the New York City area, and it has provided advanced medical training veterinarians.
2. MTA, "2021 Top Dog Award."
3. *Ibid.*
4. MTA, "The MTA Network."
5. MTA, "MTA Police Department Opens Premier Canine Training Center."
6. MTA, "2021 Top Dog Award."
7. MTA, "Five Canine Officers Complete Training Course."
8. MTA, "2021 Top Dog Award."
9. MTA, "Five Canine Officers Complete Training Course."
10. CBS, "MTA Opens State-of-the-Art K-9 Training Center."
11. MTA, "MTA Police Department Opens Premier Canine Training Center."
12. Mocker, "On Duty with K-9 Unit."
13. The Railroad Police, "History."
14. Roufa, "Railroad Police."
15. The Railroad Police, "History."
16. *Ibid.*
17. *Ibid.*
18. *Ibid.*
19. Slavik, "Building a Bond with Your K9 Partner."
20. Handy et al., "The K-9 Corps."
21. FedAgent, "The Beginning of American K9 Units."
22. Handy et al., "The K-9 Corps."
23. *Ibid.*; FedAgent, "The Beginning of American K9 Units."
24. Handy et al., "The K-9 Corps."
25. *Ibid.*
26. *Ibid.*; FedAgent, "The Beginning of American K9 Units."
27. National Academies of Sciences, Engineering, and Medicine, *K9 Units in Public Transportation*.
28. *Ibid.*, 7.
29. *Ibid.*
30. *Ibid.*

Notes—Chapter 10

31. Michigan Railroads Association, "Railroad K-9 Partners on the Job."
32. U.S. Police Canine Association Foundation, https://www.uspcak9.com/.
33. National Academies of Sciences, Engineering, and Medicine, *K9 Units in Public Transportation*, 7.
34. RJ Corman Railroad Group, "K-9 Units on the Star."
35. TSA Training Center, "TSA Canine Training Center."
36. *Ibid.*
37. *Ibid.*; American Kennel Club Staff, "2019 ACE Award Winners."
38. TSA Training Center, "TSA Canine Training Center."
39. Green, "2019 ACE Award Winner K-9 Summer."
40. American Kennel Club Staff, "2019 ACE Award Winners."
41. Green, "2019 ACE Award Winner K-9 Summer."
42. Amtrak Police Department, "K-9 Unit."
43. Young, "Meet the Adorable Dogs."
44. Amtrak Police Department, *Annual Report 2019*, 6.
45. Amtrak Police Department, "K-9 Unit"; News12 Staff, "Amtrak Officer, Dog Work Together."
46. Amtrak, "Paws for a Sec."
47. *Ibid.*
48. Amtrak, *FY 2020 Company Profile.*
49. *Ibid.*
50. Amtrak Police Department, *Annual Report 2019*, 6.
51. Amtrak, "Paws for a Sec."
52. Garner, "TSA Opens Canine Training Center."
53. Young, "Meet the Adorable Dogs."
54. Nietzel, "Auburn University Awarded $24 Million."
55. Bay Area Rapid Transit, "K9 Unit."
56. *Ibid.*
57. Bay Area Rapid Transit, "About."
58. Jordan, "From Routine Patrols to Explosives Detection."
59. Bay Area Rapid Transit, "About."
60. Metropolitan Transit Authority of Harris County, "Operations."
61. Southeastern Pennsylvania Transportation Authority, "About the Transit Police."
62. Southeastern Pennsylvania Transportation Authority, *Fiscal Year 2021 Operating Budget.*
63. Southeastern Pennsylvania Transportation Authority, "K9 Jagger to Get Body Armor."
64. BNSF Railway, "Paw-fficer on Duty."
65. *Ibid.*
66. BNSF Railway, "Fact Sheet."
67. BNSF Railway, "Paw-fficer on Duty."
68. Southeastern Pennsylvania Transportation Authority, "K9 Jagger to Get Body Armor."
69. New Jersey Transit, "K9 Unit."
70. Slavik, "Building a Bond with Your K9 Partner."
71. *Ibid.*

Chapter 10

1. Kasperowicz, "Amtrak Bill Would Let Trains Go to Dogs."
2. Associated Press, "No Pets on Amtrak Trains?"
3. *Ibid.*
4. Stein, "Dogs on Amtrak Bill."
5. Magliari, "Amtrak and Illinois DOT to Expand Pets Program."
6. *Ibid.*
7. Amtrak, "Pets on Trains, 2016."
8. Amtrak, "About Amtrak."
9. Amtrak, "All Aboard, Pets."
10. U.S. Department of Justice, "Service Animals."
11. Amtrak, "All Aboard, Pets."
12. *Ibid.*
13. Bay Area Rapid Transit, "Service Animals/Pets."
14. San Francisco Municipal Transportation Agency, "Animals on Muni."
15. PetFriendly Travel, "LIRR Pet Policy."
16. Gould and Meyer, "Lost Dog Reunited."
17. Reisen, "Traveling on the Subway with Your Dog."
18. Molloy, "Public Transport Pet Policy New York City."
19. Reisen, "Traveling on the Subway with Your Dog."
20. *Ibid.*

Notes—Chapters 11 and 12

21. U.S. Department of Justice, "Frequently Asked Questions."
22. A comprehensive list of pet policies on the U.S. railroad is available from Woof Advisor at https://www.woofadvisor.com/blog/public-transit-pet-policies-usa/.
23. Reisen, "Traveling on the Subway with Your Dog."

Chapter 11

1. Gordon, *It Takes a Dog*, 85–107.
2. Bondeson, *Amazing Dogs*, 100–03.
3. Montinari, "Lampo the Railway Dog."
4. Bondeson, *Amazing Dogs*, 102; Barlettani, *Lampo, the Traveling Dog*.
5. Montinari, "Lampo the Railway Dog."
6. Barlettani's book was originally published in Italian. It was translated by Alan Houghton Brodrick in 1963. The primary sources for this chapter include Brodrick's translation, Gordon's *It Takes a Dog*, and Bondeson's recounting of Lampo's story in *Amazing Dogs*.
7. Gordon, *It Takes a Dog*, 85–107.
8. Marquardt et al., "Stray Dogs."
9. Sternthal, "Moscow's Stray Dogs."
10. *Ibid.*
11. Boyd, "How Did Moscow's Stray Dogs Learn."
12. McGrane, "Moscow's Metro Dogs."
13. *Ibid.*
14. *Ibid.*
15. *Ibid.*
16. John, "Friday Fun."
17. McGrane, "Moscow's Metro Dogs."
18. Sternthal, "Moscow's Stray Dogs."
19. Szetei et al., "When Dogs Seem to Lose Their Nose."
20. Boyd, "How Did Moscow's Stray Dogs Learn."
21. *Ibid.*
22. Dunnell, "Compassion."
23. Macdonald, "How Moscow's 'Metro Dogs' Have Learned."

Chapter 12

1. American Veterinary Medical Association, "The Human-Animal Interaction."
2. King, *How Animals Grieve*, afterword.
3. Levin et al., "Are People More Disturbed by Dog or Human Suffering?"
4. Winch, "The Importance of Belonging to a Tribe."
5. *Ibid.*
6. Benediktová et al., "Magnetic Alignment."
7. Nahm, "Mysterious Ways."

Bibliography

Ahlbrandt, Arlene. *Annie, the Railroad Dog: "A True Story."* Fort Collins: Citizen Printing, 1998.

Ahmed, Beenish. "A Grand Central Ghost Story." *WNYC News*, October 31, 2017. https://www.wnyc.org/story/grand-central-ghost-story/.

"Albany's Columbus Day Celebration." *The Argus*, October 8, 1916, page 20. https://nyshistoricnewspapers.org.

American Kennel Club. "Bloodhound." https://www.akc.org/dog-breeds/bloodhound/. Accessed July 14, 2021.

American Kennel Club. "Scottish Terriers." akc.org/dog breeds/Scottish terrier. Accessed May 10, 2022.

American Kennel Club Staff. "2019 ACE Award Winners: Meet the 5 Heroic Dogs Being Honored This Year." September 23, 2019. https://www.akc.org/expert-advice/news/2019-ace-award-winners-meet-5-heroic-dogs-honored-year/.

American Veterinary Medical Association. "AMVA Releases Latest Stats on Pet Ownership and Veterinary Care." November 18, 2018. https://www.avma.org/News/PressRoom/Pages/-AVMA-releases-latest-stats-on-pet-ownership-and-veterinary-care.aspx.

American Veterinary Medical Association. "Human-Animal Bond." https://www.avma.org/one-health/human-animal-bond. Accessed July 14, 2021.

American Veterinary Medical Association. "The Human-Animal Interaction and Human-Animal Bond." https://www.avma.org/resources-tools/avma-policies/human-animal-interaction-and-human-animal-bond. Accessed May 15, 2022.

Amtrak. "About Amtrak." https://www.amtrak.com/about-amtrak.html. Accessed May 15, 2022.

Amtrak. "All Aboard Pets." https://www.amtrak.com/pets. Accessed May 15, 2022.

Amtrak. *FY 2020 Company Profile.* https://www.amtrak.com/content/dam/projects/dotcom/english/public/documents/corporate/nationalfactsheets/Amtrak-Company-Profile-FY2020-041921.pdf.

Amtrak. "Paws for a Sec: Meet an Amtrak Police Dog." November 2013. http://blog.amtrak.com/2013/11/amtrak-k-9/.

Amtrak. "Pets on Trains, 2016." January 22, 2016. https://history.amtrak.com/archives/pets-on-trains-2016-1.

Amtrak Police Department. *Annual Report 2019.* https://police.amtrak.com/images/2019_annual_report.pdf.

Amtrak Police Department. "K-9 Unit." 2020. https://police.amtrak.com/index.php/overview/patrol/k-9-unit.

Armstrong, G.B. *The Beginnings of the True Railway Mail Service.* Chicago: Lakeside Press, 1906.

Aronson, Steven M. "Presidential Passage." *Architectural Digest*, September 30, 2008. https://archive.architecturaldigest.com/article/2008/10/presidential-passage.

Associated Press. "Fala 'Sleeps Away'; Was Roosevelt's Pet." *New York Times*, April 6, 1952. https://www.nytimes.com/1952/04/06/archives/fala-sleeps-away-was-roosevelts-pet-fala-dies-in-sleep-pet-of.html.

Associated Press. "Lawmakers Push for Amtrak to Allow Small Pets on Trains." *Chicago Tribune*, February 17, 2015.

Bibliography

https://www.chicagotribune.com/lifestyles/chi-pets-allowed-on-amtrak-20150217-story.html?msclkid=df1229a3c27911ec91b7880f983e0ee6.

Associated Press. "No Pets on Amtrak Trains? French Bulldog-Owning Congressman Aims to Change That." *Los Angeles Daily News*, February 17, 2015. https://www.dailynews.com/2015/02/17/no-pets-on-amtrak-trains-french-bulldog-owning-congressman-aims-to-change-that/.

Association of American Railroads. "Chronology of America's Freight Railroads." April 2021. https://www.aar.org/wp-content/uploads/2020/07/AAR-Chronology-Americas-Freight-Railroads-Fact-Sheet.pdf.

Atlanta Magazine. "FDR: The Long Goodbye." August 2, 2010. https://www.atlantamagazine.com/history/fdr-the-long-goodbye1/.

Aubrey-Herzog, Jay. "Battle for Boomer Jack." *North Coast Journal*, May 31, 2007. https://www.northcoastjournal.com/humboldt/battle-for-boomer-jack/Content?oid=2125846.

Barlettani, Elvio. *Lampo il Cane Viaggiatore*. Milan, Italy: Garzanti, 1962. English edition: *Lampo, the Traveling Dog*. New York: Pantheon, 1963.

Barnes, Steve. "Train-Hopping Dog Named Railroad Jack Is Missing." *Times Union*, March 15, 2008. https://www.timesunion.com/news/article/Train-hopping-dog-from-Albany-named-Railroad-Jack-12753798.php.

Bay Area Rapid Transit. "About." https://www.bart.gov/about. Accessed May 15, 2022.

Bay Area Rapid Transit. "K9 Unit." https://www.bart.gov/about/police/people/K9. Accessed May 15, 2022.

Bay Area Rapid Transit. "Service Animals/Pets." https://www.bart.gov/guide/pets. Accessed May 15, 2022.

Beauchemin, Joseph E. "Oral History B: Railway Post Office Clerks." https://postalmuseum.si.edu/research-articles/the-railway-mail-service-oral-histories/oral-histories-b. Accessed July 14, 2021.

Benediktová, Kateřina, Jana Adámková, Jan Svoboda, Michael Scott Painter, Luděk Bartoš, Petra Nováková, Lucie Vynikalová, Vlastimil Hart, John Phillips, and Hynek Burda. "Magnetic Alignment Enhances Homing Efficiency of Hunting Dogs." *eLife* 9, e55080. https://doi.org/10.7554/eLife.55080.

Bessette, Claire. "Owney the Postal Dog Rides Again." *The Day* (New London, CT), July 28, 2013. https://www.theday.com/article/20130728/ENT18/307289988.

Betz, Bob. "Owney, the Postal Dog." *Madison County Courier*, July 24, 2011.

Beveridge, Stewart H., and Lee Nelson. *Shep: Forever Faithful*. Pleasant Grove, UT: Grove Creek Publications, 2005.

Biemiller, Carl L. *Any Friend of Owney's*. New York: Putnam, 1966.

Bishop, Jim. *FDR's Last Year*. New York: William Morrow, 1974.

Blankfield, Bryan. "'A Symbol of His Warmth and Humanity': Fala, Roosevelt, and the Personable Presidency." *Rhetoric and Public Affairs* 19, no. 2 (2016): 209–44. doi:10.14321/rhetpublaffa.19.2.0209.

Blitz, Matt. "Owney the Postal Dog Still Lives, Sort of, in DC." September 4, 2015. https://www.washingtonian.com/2015/09/04/owney-the-postal-dog-still-lives-sort-of-in-dc/

Bluebell Railway Museum. "London Jack—Collecting for the Woking Homes." https://www.bluebell-railway-museum.co.uk/images/a015.pdf. Accessed May 27, 2021.

BNSF Railway. "Fact Sheet." http://www.bnsf.com/bnsf-resources/pdf/about-bnsf/fact_sheet.pdf. Accessed May 15, 2022.

BNSF Railway. "Paw-fficer on Duty: How BNSF's K-9 Unit Helps Keep the Railroad Secure." September 25, 2019. https://www.bnsf.com/news-media/railtalk/safety/k9.html.

Bondeson, Jan. *Amazing Dogs: A Cabinet of Canine Curiosities*. Ithaca: Cornell University Press, 2011.

Boyd, Jacqueline. "How Did Moscow's Stray Dogs Learn to Navigate the Metro?" *The Conversation*, February

Bibliography

18, 2016. https://theconversation.com/how-did-moscows-stray-dogs-learn-to-navigate-the-metro-54790.

Broadway, Bill. "Poll Finds America 'as Churched as Ever.'" *Washington Post,* May 31, 1997. https://www.washingtonpost.com/archive/local/1997/05/31/poll-finds-america-as-churched-as-ever/f5e38ee3-2560-4680-b926-e2829c0c23f1/.

Cabe, Matthew. "This Desert Life: History in Your Hand." *The Daily Press,* February 17, 2017. https://www.vvdailypress.com/story/lifestyle/pets/2017/02/17/this-desert-life-history-in/22437901007/.

California Route 66 Museum. "Brownie the Railroad Dog." July 3, 2016. http://www.weirdca.com/location.php?location=320.

California Route 66 Museum. https://www.califrt66museum.org/. Accessed May 14, 2022.

California State Railroad Museum. https://www.californiarailroad.museum/. Accessed May 14, 2022.

"A Canine King." *The Morning Call* (San Francisco, CA), April 20, 1893, page 3, col. 5. https://bit.ly/3rjRiPn.

Carter, Elliott. "Ferdinand Magellan Presidential Railcar." *Atlas Obscura,* January 5, 2017. https://www.atlasobscura.com/places/ferdinand-magellan.

CBS. "MTA Opens State-of-the-Art K-9 Training Center." June 8, 2016. https://www.cbsnews.com/newyork/news/mta-canine-training-facility/.

City of Fort Collins. "Operation Services." fcgov/observer/transit-center.php. Accessed July 14, 2021.

Cleaver, Shandos. "How to Travel on Amtrak Trains with a Dog in 2022." *Travelnuity,* January 6, 2022. https://www.travelnuity.com/travelling-on-amtrak-with-a-dog/#:~:text=On%2DBoard%20the%20Train%20with%20a%20Pet&text=Once%20you've%20found%20seats,than%20the%20seat%20in%20front.

Collard, Sneed B., III. *Shep, Our Most Loyal Dog.* Ann Arbor: Sleeping Bear Press, 2006.

Coloradoan. "The Tale of Annie the Railroad Dog" [Podcast, Episode 13]. *The Way It Was.* https://www.coloradoan.com/series/thewayitwas/.

Coloradoan Staff. "10 Events That Shaped Fort Collins History." *Coloradoan,* May 30, 2014. https://www.coloradoan.com/story/announcements/2014/05/30/events-helped-shape-fort-collins-history/9766921/.

Coppinger, L., and R. Coppinger. "Dogs for Herding and Guarding Livestock," in *Livestock Handling and Transport,* ed. T. Grandin. Wallingford, UK: CAB International, 2000, 235–54.

Curious Wanderer. "Boomer Jacks: The Northwestern Pacific's (NWP) Railroad Dog." 2019. https://www.curiouswanderer.com/post/boomer-jacks-the-northwestern-pacific-s-nwp-railroad-dog.

Cushing, Marshall. *The Story of Our Post Office: The Greatest Government Department in All Its Phases.* Boston: A.M. Thayer, 1893.

Dennis, W.J. *The Traveling Post Office.* Des Moines: The Homestead Printing Co., 1916.

"Depot Dog's Memory Lives." *The Denver Post,* May 23, 2008. https://www.denverpost.com/2008/05/23/depot-dogs-memory-lives/.

"Dog a Real Sherlock Holmes." *Washington Post,* November 12, 1911. https://www.newspapers.com/newspage/31553715/.

"The Dog Owney Dead at Last." *Tacoma Daily News,* June 12, 1897.

"Dog Tourist Owney." *The Evening World* (New York, NY), April 26, 1892, Extra Last Edition, page 2, col. 1.

"A Dog with Many Masters." *New York Times,* July 9, 1911, page 5.

Dows, Olin. *Franklin Roosevelt at Hyde Park.* New York: American Artists Group, 1949.

Dunnell, Tony. "Compassion, Moscow, Russia." *Atlas Obscura,* May 20, 2019. https://www.atlasobscura.com/places/compassion-malchik-monument.

Experience First. "History of the Haunted Subways of New York City." October 12, 2016. https://www.exp1.com/blog/untold-nyc-history-haunted-subways/.

Bibliography

"Fala Buried in Hyde Park Garden at Feet of Friend and Champion." *New York Times,* April 6, 1952. https://www.nytimes.com/1952/04/07/archives/fala-buried-in-hyde-park-garden-at-feet-of-friend-and-champion.html.

"Fala Present at Burial of Master at Hyde Park." *Baltimore Sun,* April 16, 1945, page 5.

FedAgent. "The Beginning of American K9 Units: A Brief History." August 22, 2019. https://www.fedagent.com/news/the-beginning-of-american-k9-units-a-brief-history.

Fort Collins History Connection. "Annie the Railroad Dog." https://history.fcgov.com/explore/annie#:~:text=When%20railroad%20brakeman%20Chris%20Demuth,She%20died%20in%201948. Accessed June 15, 2021.

Fort Collins Museum of Discovery. "Daily Discovery: Annie the Railroad Dog." May 10, 2020. https://fcmod.org/blog/2020/05/10/daily-discovery-annie-the-railroad-dog/.

Franklin D. Roosevelt Presidential Library and Museum. Telegram from Funeral Train to White House, Greenville, SC, April 13, 1945. Office of Social Entertainment File.

Fritz, Harry W. "The Railroads Transformed Montana." University of Montana Department of History. http://www.umt.edu/this-is-montana/columns/stories/the-railroad-transformed-montana.php. Accessed April 8, 2019.

Gallagher, Hugh Gregory. *FDR's Splendid Deception.* New York: Dodd and Mead, 1985.

The Garda Post, "Early Days of Railroad Policing to Present," https://garda-post.com/early-days-of-railroad-policing-to-present/.

Garner, Marissa. "TSA Opens Canine Training Center at JBSA-Lackland." March 9, 2016. https://www.aetc.af.mil/News/Article-Display/Article/689331/tsa-opens-canine-training-center-at-jbsa-lackland/.

Gavan, Peggy. "1904: Roxy the Long Island Railroad Mascot Dog with an Unlimited Commuter Train Pass." May 20, 2018. http://hatchingcatnyc.com/2018/05/20/roxy-long-island-railroad-dog/.

Gavan, Peggy. "1908: The Dog Detectives of the Long Island Railroad Police Force."April 4, 2015. https://hatchingcatnyc.com/tag/shebas-bob/.

Gibbons, Caitlan. "Fort Collins Library Ends 'Annie Walk.'" *The Denver Post,* July 9, 2011. https://www.denverpost.com/2011/07/09/fort-collins-library-ends-annie-walk/.

Goodwin, Doris Kearns. *No Ordinary Time: Franklin and Eleanor Roosevelt: The Home Front in World War II.* New York: Simon & Schuster, 1994. Kindle edition.

Gordon, Kevin. "Railway Jack." *Quirky Sussex History,* November 26, 2019. https://sussexhistory.net/2019/11/26/railway-jack/.

Gordon, Ruth. *It Takes a Dog to Raise a Village: True Stories of Remarkable Canine Vagabonds* Minocqua, WI: Willow Creek Press, 2000.

Gould, Jennifer, and David Meyer. "Lost Dog Reunited with His Owner by LIRR Crew that Found Him on Tracks." *New York Post,* March 12, 2021. https://nypost.com/2021/03/12/lost-dog-reunited-with-his-owner-by-lirr-crew-that-found-him-on-tracks/.

Grant, H. Roger. *Railroads and the American People.* Bloomington: Indiana University Press, 2012.

Great American Stations. "Victorville, CA (VRV)." https://www.greatamericanstations.com/stations/victorville-ca-vrv/. Accessed July 25, 2021.

Great Northern Railways Historical Society. "Great Northern History." http://www.gnrhs.org/gn_history.php. Accessed April 26, 2019.

"The Greatest of Dog Detectives." *The Medina Daily Journal,* November 8, 1911, page 2. https://nyshistoricnewspapers.org/.

Green, Ranny. "2019 ACE Award Winner K-9 Summer the Labrador Retriever Helps Keep D.C. Safe." American Kennel Club, November 14, 2019. https://www.akc.org/expert-advice/news/uniformed-k9-vet-lab-summer-wins-2019-ace-award/.

Bibliography

Griffin, Taylor Chastain. "Combating Social Isolation and Loneliness Through the Human Animal Bond." *Pet Partners Interactions Magazine* (Spring 2021): 10.

Handy, William F., Marilyn Harrington, and David J. Pittman. "The K-9 Corps: The Use of Dogs in Police Work." *The Journal of Criminal Law, Criminology, and Police Science* 52, no. 3 (September 1961): 328–37.

Hassett, William D. *Off the Record with FDR 1942–1945*. New Brunswick: Rutgers University Press, 1958.

Hatch, Alden. *Franklin D. Roosevelt: An Informal Biography*. Whitefish, MT: Kessinger, 2005.

Hatching Cat of Gotham. https://hatchingcatnyc.com/tag/shebas-bob/ retrieved. Accessed September 1, 2022.

"He Was a Baggage Car Dog." *New York Times,* June 16, 1893. https://www.nytimes.com/1893/06/16/archives/he-was-a-baggagecar-dog-incidents-in-the-remarkable-career-of.html.

Hebert, Lou. *The Hidden History of Toledo*. Charleston, SC: The History Press, 2019.

Hebert, Lou. "Owney the Famous Postal Dog Met His Tragic Demise in Toledo." *The Toledo Gazette,* July 26, 2011. https://toledogazette.wordpress.com/2011/07/26/owney-the-famous-postal-dog-met-his-tragic-demise-in-toledo/.

Herzog, Hal. "Encounters with Dead Pets: A Study of the Evolution of Grief." *Psychology Today,* June 17, 2015. https://www.psychologytoday.com/us/blog/animals-and-us/201506/encounters-dead-pets-study-the-evolution-grief.

Hingston, Sandy. "11 Things You Might Not Know About Owney, the Post Office Dog." *Philadelphia,* July 27, 2016. https://www.phillymag.com/news/2016/07/27/owney-post-office-dog-john-wanamaker/.

History.com. "This Day in History: FDR Defends His Dog in a Speech." November 16, 2009. https://www.history.com/this-day-in-history/fdr-defends-his-dog.

HistoryColorado.org. "Colorado and Southern Freight Depot." April 1, 2001. https://www.historycolorado.org/grant-news/2001/04/01/colorado-southern-freight-depot.

Holder, Charles Frederick. "Owney's Trip Around the World." *St. Nicholas: An Illustrated Magazine for Young Folks* 23, no. 9 (July 1896), 720–724. https://ufdc.ufl.edu/UF00065513/00313/6x.

"How Roxey Became a Long Island Pet." *The South Side Signal,* July 3, 1914. http://nyshistoricnewspapers.org.

Huggins, Kelli. "Finding Railroad Jack." https://findingrailroadjack.com/. Accessed July 14, 2021.

Humane Education Coalition. https://www.hecoalition.org. Accessed July 14, 2021.

Inbody, Kristen. "16 Years Honoring Shep's Story." *Great Falls Tribune,* March 16, 2017. https://www.greatfallstribune.com/story/life/my-montana/2017/03/16/years-honoring-shep-story/99278354/.

"Inspector Owney Here." *New-York Tribune,* July 1, 1896, page 14, col. 2.

Insurance Information Institute. "Pet Statistics." https://www.iii.org/fact-statistic/facts-statistics-pet-statistics. Accessed April 10, 2019.

John, Vineet. "Friday Fun: Moscow Metro's Commuter Dogs." *The City Fix,* March 28, 2014. https://thecityfix.com/blog/friday-fun-moscow-metros-commuter-dogs-vineet-john/.

Jones, Danielle. "The True Story of the Coolest Dog the White House Has Ever Seen." *Bark Post,* January 8, 2014. https://barkpost.com/life/world-leaders-their-dogs.

Jordan, Melissa. "From Routine Patrols to Explosives Detection, K-9 Unit Helps Keep BART Riders Safe." May 11, 2010. https://www.bart.gov/news/articles/2010/news20100511.

Kalmbach Books. *The Historical Guide to North American Railroads*, 3rd ed. Waukesha: Kalmbach Books, 2014.

Kasperowicz, Pete. "Amtrak Bill Would Let Trains Go to Dogs." *The Hill,* May 22, 2013. https://thehill.com/blogs/floor-action/house/151294-new-bill-would-let-dogs-and-cats-on-amtrak/.

Kelly, Kate. "Fala, FDR's Beloved Dog." *America Comes Alive.* https://america

Bibliography

comesalive.com/fala-best-known-presidential-dog/. Accessed July 16, 2021.

Kerby, Mona. *Owney, the Mail Pouch Pooch* [Video]. 2007. https://www.youtube.com/watch?v=SyioQlIIDeE.

Kerby, Mona. *Owney, the Mail Pouch Pooch*. New York: Farrar, Straus and Giroux, 2008.

Kilian, Lincoln. *Boomer Jack of the Northwestern Pacific*. Mendocino County Museum Grassroots History Publication, 2005.

King, Barbara K. *How Animals Grieve*. Chicago: University of Chicago Press, 2013.

Kinsolving, Kathleen. *The Dogs of War*. New York: WND Books, 2012. Kindle edition.

Klara, Robert. *FDR's Funeral Train*. New York: St. Martin's Press, 2010. Kindle edition.

Kluckholn, Frank. "Crowds in Tears at Rail Station Watch Funeral Train Roll North." *New York Times*, April 14, 1945, page 4.

Lang, Sandy. "Dog's Gravestone Has Nine Lives." *Triangle Review News*, May 12, 1997, page 1.

Lengel, E.G. "Franklin D. Roosevelt's Train Ferdinand Magellan." White House Historical Association, October 19, 2017. https://www.whitehousehistory.org/franklin-d-roosevelt-rsquo-s-train-ferdinand-magellan.

Levin, Jack, Arnold Arluke, and Leslie Irvine. "Are People More Disturbed by Animal or Human Suffering?" *Society and Animals* 25, no. 1 (April 2017): 1–16.

Library of Congress. "Owney, the Railway Mail Dog: Topics in Chronicling America." https://guides.loc.gov/chronicling-america-owney-the-railroad-dog. Accessed May 1, 2021.

Lindeblade, Carl. "Roosevelt Funeral Train." *C-SPAN*, August 7, 2013. https://www.c-span.org/video/?-314427-1/roosevelt-funeral-train.

"LIRR Thieves Caught with Bloodhounds' Aid." *Brooklyn Daily Eagle*, August 1911, page 15. https://bklyn.newspapers.com/clip/45983015/-kerkams-bloodhounds-lirr-theives/.

Llewellyn, John. "Paws, Pathos, and Presidential Persuasion: Franklin Roosevelt's 'Fala Speech' as Precursor and Model for Richard Nixon's 'Checkers Speech.'" *Communication and Theater Association of Minnesota Journal* 37 (2010): 64–75.

Long, B.A. *Mail by Rail: The Story of the Postal Transportation System*. New York: Simmons-Boardman, 1951.

"Looking Back." *Toledo Blade*, June 1897. https://c6edddca-e5f7-4608-a341-569d3a0780f7.filesusr.com/ugd/b3a8f7_7207758feede406194922f2eaf8bb478.pdf.

Macdonald, Cheyenne. "How Moscow's 'Metro Dogs' Have Learned to Navigate the City's Subways." *Daily Mail Online*, March 21, 2016. www.dailymail.co.uk/sciencetech/-article-3503544/How-Moscow-s-metro-dogs-learned-navigate-city-s-subways-Canine-senses-help-master-complex-routes-claims-scientist.html.

Magliari, M. "Amtrak and Illinois DOT to Expand Pets Program to a Second Downstate Route." AMTRAK press release, August 2, 2014. https://media.amtrak.com/2014/08/amtrak-and-illinois-dot-to-expand-pets-program-to-a-second-downstate-route/.

Marquardt, Alex, Bill Blakemore, and Ross Eichenholz. "Stray Dogs Master Complex Moscow Subway System." ABC News, March 19, 2010. shorturl.at/jnrZ5.

Martin, Timothy. *Somewhere Down the Line: The Legend of Boomer Jack*. Miami: Neverland, 2013.

McGann, Tom. "Funeral of the Famous: Franklin Delano Roosevelt—Part II." *American Funeral Director* (September 1992): 27.

McGrane, Sally. "Moscow's Metro Dogs." *The New Yorker*, July 8, 2013. https://www.newyorker.com/culture/culture-desk/moscows-metro-dogs.

McMillan, Bob. "The Herd Dog Who Became a Montana Legend." *The Wildstare*, June 5, 2018.

Metropolitan Transit Authority of Harris County. "Operations." https://ridemetro.org/Pages/METRO%20Police%20Operations.aspx.

Michigan Railroads Association.

Bibliography

"Railroad K-9 Partners on the Job." *MRA Rail Update* (Fall 2014), 1, 4. https://pdfsecret.com/queue/-fall-2014-michigan-railroads-association_5a2fd5cad64ab21cdb5e7078_pdf?queue_id=-1.

Middleton, William D. *Grand Central: The World's Greatest Railway Terminal.* San Marino, CA: Golden West Books, 1977.

Middleton, William D. *Manhattan Gateway: New York's Pennsylvania Station.* Waukesha: Kalmbach Books, 1997.

Mocker, Greg. "On Duty with K-9 Unit at Grand Central Terminal." *Pix11*, December 15, 2017. https://pix11.com/news/on-duty-with-k-9-unit-at-grand-central-terminal/.

Molloy, G. "Public Transport Pet Policy New York City." *Woof Advisor.* https://www.woofadvisor.com/blog/travelling-with-your-dog-on-public-transport-new-york/. Accessed May 15, 2022.

Monroe, Herbert. "President's Special." *Railroad* (November 1945): 19.

Montana Kids. "The Story of Shep." http://montanakids.com/cool_stories/Famous_Montanans/shep.htm. Accessed April 26, 2019.

Montinari, Giulia. "Lampo the Railway Dog: The Friendly Mutt Who Traveled All Over Italy by Train." *History of Yesterday*, September 6, 2020. https://historyofyesterday.com/lampo-the-railway-dog-e4e4f39d1c8c.

Moon, Ellie. "Gravestone Stands as Tribute to Brownie the Railroad Dog." *The Daily Press*, 1960s (date unknown), as shown on http://www.weirdca.com/location.php?location=320.

Morgan, D.P. *Fast Mail, the First 75 Years: A History of the Burlington Railroad's Mail Service Between Chicago and Council Bluffs—Omaha, 1884–1959.* Mobile Post Office Society, 1959.

MTA. "Five Canine Officers Complete MTA PD Anti-terrorism Training Course." *Mass Transit*, February 10, 2020. https://www.masstransitmag.com/safety-security/training-testing-services/press-release/21124912/mta-headquarters-five-canine-officers-complete-mta-pd-antiterrorism-training-course.

MTA. "The MTA Network." https://new.mta.info/about-us/the-mta-network. Accessed May 22, 2022.

MTA. "MTA Police Department Opens Premier Canine Training Center." *Mass Transit*, June 9, 2016. https://www.masstransitmag.com/safety-security/press-release/12218831/metropolitan-transportation-authority-ny-mta-mta-police-department-opens-premier-canine-training-center.

MTA. "MTA Police Department's Canine Unit Receives 2021 Top Dog Award." Press Release, December 15, 2021. https://new.mta.info/press-release/-mta-police-departments-canine-unit-receives-2021-top-dog-award.

MTA. "Only Mass Transit Oriented Police Canine Training Facility in the United States." June 8, 2016. https://www.mta.info/news-k-9-mtapd-mta-police/2016/06/08/only-mass-transit-oriented-police-canine-training-facility?fbclid=IwAR3ZYjzRf-eH609BazDRUcepqdq-BhE-0gcgyowBQ7fJ0hdnmv0HP41N2oY.

"Much Traveled Dog." *The Morning Times* (Washington, D.C.), March 15, 1896, part 3, page 22, col. 6.

Nahm, Michael. "Mysterious Ways: The Riddle of the Homing Ability in Dogs and Other Vertebrates." *Journal of the Society for Psychical Research* 79 no. 3 (July 2015): 140–155.

National Academies of Sciences, Engineering, and Medicine. *K9 Units in Public Transportation: A Guide for Decision Makers.* Washington, D.C.: The National Academies Press, 2002. https://doi.org/10.17226/24721.

National Archives. "Forward with Roosevelt." September 22, 2010. https://fdr.blogs.archives.gov/2010/09/22/-this-week-in-roosevelt-history-september-22-30/.

National Historic Route 66 Federation. "Route 66 History." https://national66.org/pages/route-66-history. Accessed May 14, 2022.

National Park Service. "Fala." https://www.nps.gov/articles/fala.htm. Accessed May 11, 2022.

New Jersey Transit. "K9 Unit." https://

Bibliography

police.njtransit.com/bureaus/operations/special/K9. Accessed May 15, 2022.

Nietzel, Michael T. "Auburn University Awarded $24 Million to Study, Train Counterterrorism Dogs." *Forbes*, March 15, 2022. https://www.forbes.com/sites/michaeltnietzel/2022/03/15/auburn-university-awarded-24-million-to-train-counterterrorism-dogs/?sh=cd3278d3ba4a.

Northwestern Pacific Railroad Historical Society, "NWP Railroad History." Last updated May 16, 2011. http://www.nwprrhs.org/history.html.

"Owney a Great Traveler." *New York Times*, December 24, 1895.

"Owney Bobs Up Again." *San Francisco Call*, April 28, 1897, page 3, col. 7.

"'Owney' in a Connecticut Town." *The Sun* (New York, NY), January 7, 1891, page 8, col. 3. https://chroniclingamerica.loc.gov/lccn/sn83030272/1891-01-07/ed-1/seq-8/.

"Owney Is a Dead Dog." *Los Angeles Times*, June 13, 1897.

"Owney Is on Exhibition." *The Times* (Washington, D.C.), January 27, 1898, page 1, col. 7.

"Owney: Postal Railway Mascot." *Genealogy Trails*. http://genealogytrails.com/ny/albany/bio_owney.html. Accessed July 14, 2021.

"Owney, the Dog: He Has Traveled Almost Around the World," *The Roanoke Daily Times*, July 24, 1896. https://bit.ly/3wNSM5y.

"Owney, the Famous Tramp Dog." *The Big Stone Gap Post* (Big Stone Gap, VA), April 6, 1893, page 1, col. 6.

"Owney the Tramp Dog." *The Record-Union* (Sacramento, CA), August 4, 1899, page 5, col. 2.

"Owney Was Here." *Daily Public Ledger* (Maysville, KY), September 3, 1894, page 1.

"Pagan Beliefs Persist in the New World." *Economist*, October 31, 2018. https://www.economist.com/graphic-detail/2018/10/31/pagan-beliefs-persist-in-the-new-world.

Paine, S.H. "Owney's Travels: On the Home-Stretch of a Round-the World Tour." *Los Angeles Times*, December 25, 1895, page 1. https://www.proquest.com/docview/163785236.

Paine, S.H. "Story of the U.S. Mail." *Railroad Man's Magazine* 33, no. 3 (1917).

Parkinson, Justin. "The Dead Dog That Changed Color Twice." *BBC News Magazine*, July 30, 2014. https://www.bbc.com/news/magazine-28420246.

"The Passing of Roxey." *The Sun* (New York, NY), June 13, 1914, page 6.

PBS. *The Rise and Fall of Penn Station* [Video]. 2014. https://www.pbs.org/wgbh/americanexperience/films/penn/.

PetFriendly Travel. "LIRR Pet Policy—Pets on Long Island Railroad." https://petfriendlytravel.com/pft_trains/new-york-mta-long-island-rail-road-lirr-pet-policy/. Accessed May 15, 2022.

Phillips, Tony. "Boomer Jack–The Northwestern Pacific's (NWP) Railroad Dog." https://www.mendotraintony.com/category/nwp-northwestern-pacific-railroad/. Accessed July 14, 2021.

"Police Department: Meet the Famous L.I.R.R. Platform Squad." *Long Island Railroad Information Bulletin*, September 30, 1924. https://www.arrts-arrchives.com/LIPDept.html.

Pope, Nancy. "The Post Office's Best Friend: Owney the Mail Dog." *Postmaster Advocate* 117 (2011): 48–52.

Pope, Nancy A. "Braving the Rails: U.S. Railway Mail Clerks from 1890–1905." *NPC News* 1, no. 3 (1989): 19–36.

Presidential Pet Museum. "FDR's Famous Scottish Terrier, Fala." July 22, 2013. https://www.presidentialpetmuseum.com/pets/fala/.

Pressler, Margaret Webb. "Owney the Postal Dog Delivers." *Washington Post*, July 25, 2011.

"Queer Tales from Nature's Book." *The Times* (Washington, D.C.), March 14, 1897.

"Railroad Jack Dead." *Ticonderoga Sentinel*, August 16, 1906, page 1. https://nyshistoricnewspapers.org/lccn/sn93063544/1906-08-16/ed-1/seq-1.pdf.

"Railroad Jack Is Dead." *The Johnstown Daily Republican*, July 31, 1906, page 2.

"Railroad Jack Kidnapped." *The Evening*

Bibliography

News, October 16, 1891, page 3. nyhistoricnewspapers.org.

"Railroad Jack on a Tour to the Pacific Coast." *The Plattsburgh Sentinel*, July 29, 1892, page 8. https://nyshistoricnewspapers.org/lccn/sn85026976/1892-07-29/ed-1/seq-8/.

"Railroad Jack Stolen." *Ogdensburg Journal*, October 17, 1891.

The Railroad Police. "History." http://www.therailroadpolice.com/history. Accessed July 14, 2021.

Railroad Police. "History." http://www.therailroadpolice.com/history. Accessed May 15, 2022.

Railtown Staff. "Buster and Hobo—the Sierra Railway Dogs." Railtown 1897 State Historic Park, September 24, 2014. https://railtown1897.wordpress.com/2014/09/24/buster-and-hobo-the-sierra-railway-dogs/.

"Railway Jack." *Sussex Agricultural Express*, July 29, 1932. https://www.britishnewspaperarchive.co.uk/search/results?basicsearch=railway%20jack&retrievecoun.

Rees, Jerry, and Stephen Michael Schwartz. *Owney: Tales from the Rails* [Video]. Washington, D.C.: Smithsonian National Postal Museum, 2018. https://www.si.edu/es/object/yt_akz0k7JNEdY.

Reisen, Jan. "Traveling on the Subway with Your Dog: What You Should Know." American Kennel Club, May 24, 2018. https://www.akc.org/expert-advice/home-living/dogs-on-the-subway/?msclkid=b851184cc0e511ecab8c70bcbbdbd5a5.

River and Plains Society. *Man's Best Friend: The Story of Shep* [Booklet]. Fort Benton, MT: River and Plains Society, not dated.

RJ Corman Railroad Group. "K-9 Units on the Star." August 9, 2019. https://www.rjcorman.com/newsroom/news-articles/k9-units-star.

Roadside America. "Owney, the Dog Postal Mascot." https://www.roadsideamerica.com/story/3624. Accessed July 14, 2021.

Roadside America. "Roadside Grave of Roxey the Railroad Dog." https://www.roadsideamerica.com/story/35888. Accessed July 14, 2021.

Robinson, Ken. "Shep Eternal: The Magical Life and Afterlife of Our World Famous Faithful Dog." *The Great Falls Tribune*, January 11, 2022. https://www.greatfallstribune.com/story/news/2022/01/11/the-magical-legacy-of-fort-bentons-faithful-dog-shep/53234774007/.

Romanski, F.J. "The Fast Mail: A History of the US Railway Mail Service." *Prologue Magazine* (Fall 2005): 1–6.

Roosevelt, Eleanor. *The Autobiography of Eleanor Roosevelt*. New York: Harper-Collins, 2014. Kindle edition.

Roosevelt, Eleanor. "My Day, December 16, 1941." *The Eleanor Roosevelt Papers Digital Edition* (2017). https://www2.gwu.edu/~erpapers/myday/displaydocedits.cfm?_y=1941&_f=md056057. Accessed May 11, 2022.

Roosevelt, Eleanor. *On My Own: The Years Since the White House*. Auckland: Pickle Partners, 1959. Kindle edition.

Rosenman, Samuel J. *Working with Roosevelt*. New York: Harper, 1952.

Roufa, Timothy. "Railroad Police and Special Agent Job Information." March 6, 2019. https://www.thebalancecareers.com/railroad-police-and-special-agent-job-information-974842.

Rowan, Roy, and Brooke Janis. *First Dogs: American Presidents and Their Best Friends*. Chapel Hill: Algonquin Books, 1997.

"Roxey's Appeal." *The County Review*, October 10, 1913, page 12. http://nyshistoricnewspapers.org.

Ruddell, Rick, and Scott Decker. "Train Robbery: A Retrospective Look at an Obsolete Crime." *Criminal Justice Review* 42, no. 4 (2017): 333–348. doi:10.1177/0734016817702192.

Sackler, Jill. "The True Story of Roxey—the Official Long Island Railroad Mascot." *Active Rain*, February 9, 2011. https://activerain.com/blogsview/2127977/the-true.

San Francisco Municipal Transportation Agency. "Animals on Muni." https://www.sfmta.com/getting-around/accessibility/muni/animals-

Bibliography

muni#:~:text=Pet%20Policy&text=Dogs%20must%20be%20leashed%20and,for%20their%20pet%20to%20ride. Accessed May 15, 2022.

Saraniero, Nicole. "A Memorial to Roxey: The Canine Mascot of the Long Island Railroad." *Untapped Cities*, May 25, 2018. https://untappedcities.com/2018/05/25/a-memorial-to-roxey-the-canine-mascot-of-the-long-island-railroad/.

Schlichting, Kurt. *Grand Central Terminal: Railroads, Engineering and Architecture in New York City*. Baltimore: Johns Hopkins University Press, 2001.

"Second Railroad Jack Killed." *Poughkeepsie Evening Enterprise*, July 26, 1897, page 4.

Sherwood, Robert E. *Roosevelt and Hopkins*. New York: Harper, 1948.

Slavik, Don. "Building a Bond with Your K9 Partner." U.S. Police Canine Association, October 23, 2020. https://www.uspcak9.com/index.php?option=com_dailyplanetblog&view=entry&year=2020&month=10&day=23&id=21:building-a-bond-with-your-K9-partner.

Smithsonian National Postal Museum. "Art of the Stamp: Owney." https://postalmuseum.si.edu/exhibition/art-of-the-stamp-owney. Accessed July 14, 2021.

Smithsonian National Postal Museum. "The Creation, 1832–1864." https://postalmuseum.si.edu/research-articles/the-railway-mail-service-history-of-the-service/the-creation-1832-1864. Accessed July 14, 2021.

Smithsonian National Postal Museum. "Dangers on the Rail." https://postalmuseum.si.edu/research-articles/the-railway-mail-service/danger-on-the-rail. Accessed July 14, 2021.

Smithsonian National Postal Museum. "A Day in the Life of a Railway Post Office Clerk." https://postalmuseum.si.edu/research-articles/the-railway-mail-service/a-day-in-the-life-of-a-railway-post-office-clerk. Accessed July 14, 2021.

Smithsonian National Postal Museum. "Decades of Change, 1920s–1950s." https://postalmuseum.si.edu/research-articles/the-railway-mail-service-history-of-the-service/decades-of-change-1920s-1950s. Accessed July 14, 2021.

Smithsonian National Postal Museum. "Expansion and Turmoil, 1876–1920." https://postalmuseum.si.edu/research-articles/the-railway-mail-service-history-of-the-service/expansion-and-turmoil-1876-1920/. Accessed July 14, 2021.

Smithsonian National Postal Museum. "A Fast Start, 1864–1875." https://postalmuseum.si.edu/research-articles/the-railway-mail-service-history-of-the-service/a-fast-start-1864-1875. Accessed July 14, 2021.

Smithsonian National Postal Museum. "The Final Run, 1960s–1977." https://postalmuseum.si.edu/research-articles/the-railway-mail-service-history-of-the-service/the-final-run-1960s-1977. Accessed July 14, 2021.

Smithsonian National Postal Museum. "Owney Silver Spoon." https://postalmuseum.si.edu/object/npm_2005.2007.1. Accessed July 14, 2021.

Smithsonian National Postal Museum. "Owney the Dog." https://www.postalmuseum.si.edu/exhibition/about-postal-operations-popular-culture-seals-symbols/owney-the-dog. Accessed July 14, 2021.

Smithsonian National Postal Museum. "Owney: Topical Reference Page." https://postalmuseum.si.edu/owney. Accessed July 14, 2021.

Smithsonian National Postal Museum. "Railway Mail Service." https://postalmuseum.si.edu/topics/railway-mail-service. Accessed July 14, 2021.

Smithsonian National Postal Museum. *Story of Owney, Mascot of the Railway Mail Service* [Video]. 2009. https://www.youtube.com/watch?v=JKar7eU3VAs.

Smithsonian National Postal Museum. "Story of Owney." https://postalmuseumsi.edu/museum-highlight/story-of-owney. Accessed July 14, 2021.

Southeastern Pennsylvania Transportation

Bibliography

Authority. "About the Transit Police." https://www5.septa.org/about/security/about-septa-police/. Accessed July 10, 2022.

Southeastern Pennsylvania Transportation Authority. *Fiscal Year 2021 Operating Budget.* https://planning.septa.org/wp-content/uploads/2021/02/-Operating-Budget-FY2021.pdf.

Southeastern Pennsylvania Transportation Authority. "SEPTA Transit Police Department's K9 Jagger to Get Body Armor." September 5, 2017. https://www.facebook.com/septaphilly/posts/septa-transit-police-departments-k9-jagger-to-get-body-armorsepta-transit-police/1903981019618191/?_rdr.

Stark, Lisa. "Dogs: The Furry, Faithful Secret Weapons of WWII." *ABC News,* November 29, 2012. https://abcnews.go.com/blogs/politics/2012/11/dogs-the-furry-faithful-secret-weapons-of-wwii.

Stein, Sam. "Dogs on Amtrak Bill Would Allow Pets on Trains." *Huffington Post,* May 22, 2013. https://www.huffpost.com/entry/dogs-on-amtrak_n_3320655?msclkid=5cbd2b0ac27a11ec88dbd403bbc8456a.

Steinbeck, John. *The Grapes of Wrath.* New York: Penguin, 1939: chapter 12, page 118.

Sternthal, Susanne. "Moscow's Stray Dogs." *Financial Times,* January 16, 2010. https://web.archive.org/web/20111216133637/http://www.ft.com/cms/s/0/628a8500-ff1c-11de-a677-00144feab49a.html.

Stevens, Walter Barlow. *Missouri, the Center State, Volume 1: 1821–1915.* Chicago: S.J. Clarke, 1915.

"Story of a Canine Wanderer." *Chicago Daily Tribune,* March 13, 1891.

Stover, John F. *American Railroads.* Chicago: University of Chicago Press, 1961.

Suckley, Daisy, and Alice Dalgliesh. *The True Story of Fala.* Delmar, NY: Black Dome Press Corp., 1942.

Suckley, Margaret. *Closest Companion: The Unknown Story of the Intimate Relationship Between Franklin Roosevelt and Margaret Suckley.* Ed. Geoffrey C. Ward. Boston: Houghton Mifflin, 1995.

Szetei, V., Á. Miklósi, J. Topál, and V. Csányi. "When Dogs Seem to Lose Their Nose: An Investigation on the Use of Visual and Olfactory Cues in Communicative Context Between Dog and Owner." *Applied Animal Behaviour Science* 83, no. 2 (2003): 141–152.

"Toledo Police Museum." *The Bulletin* (Oregon), August 21, 1963. https://c6edddca-e5f7-4608-a341-569d3a0780f7.filesusr.com/ugd/b3a8f7_7207758feede406194922f2eaf8bb478.pdf.

Toledo Police Museum. "Owney, the Postal Dog Wonder." https://www.toledopolicemuseum.com/owney-the-postal-dog-wonder. Accessed July 14, 2021.

"Travels of a Dog." *Perrysburg Journal* (Perrysburg, OH), April 7, 1894, page 2, col. 1.

TSA. "TSA Canine Training Center." May 19, 2021. https://www.tsa.gov/news/press/factsheets/tsa-canine-training-center.

Tully, Grace. *FDR: My Boss.* San Francisco: Papamoa Press, 2017. Kindle edition.

Tuolumne County Historical Society. "Railroad Transportation." http://tchistory.org/railroad-transportation/. Accessed May 14, 2022.

News12 Staff. "Amtrak Officer, Dog Work Together to Keep Penn Station Safe." September 4, 2008. https://bronx.news12.com/amtrak-officer-dog-work-together-to-keep-penn-station-safe-39018080.

University of Nebraska Lincoln. "The Great Plains During World War II." 2008. http://plainshumanities.unl.edu/homefront/thehomefront.html?section=homefront.

U.S. Department of Justice. "Frequently Asked Questions about Service Animals and the ADA." July 2015. https://www.ada.gov/regs2010/service_animal_qa.html.

U.S. Department of Justice. "Service Animals." Last modified February 24, 2020. https://www.ada.gov/service_animals_2010.htm.

U.S. Post Office Department. *Annual Report of the Postmaster-General.* Post

Bibliography

Office Department. Washington, D.C.: Government Printing Office, 1856–1977.

U.S. Post Office Department. *History of the Railway Mail Service: A Chapter in the History of Postal Affairs in the United States*. Washington, D.C.: Government Printing Office, 1885.

U.S. Postal Service. *The United States Postal Service: An American History*. Washington, D.C.: U.S. Postal Service, 2020. https://about.usps.com/publications/pub100.pdf.

Victorville. "About Victorville." https://www.victorvilleca.gov/our-city/about-victorville. Accessed May 14, 2022.

Visit Tuolumne County. "Tuolumne County Facts." https://www.visittuolumne.com/tuolumne-county-facts. Accessed May 14, 2022.

Wales, Dirk. *A Lucky Dog: Owney, U.S. Rail Mail Mascot*. Chicago: Great Plains Press, 2003.

Wallick, Rebecca. "Dogs on Trains? Yes, If a Proposed Amtrak Bill Passes." *The Bark*, May 2013. Last modified August 2021. https://thebark.com/content/-dogs-trains?page=show&msclkid=4c4e8a74c27811eca2fb3682d838a90f.

Warnick, Ron. "Dog's Grave Marker Moved to Route 66 Museum." *Route 66 News*, January 24, 2008. www.route66news.com/2008/01/24/dogs-grave-marker-moved-to-route-66-museum.

Watrous, Ansell. *The History of Larimer County*. Fort Collins: Courier Printing and Publishing, 1911.

Waymarking.com. "Brownie the Railroad Dog." https://www.waymarking.com/waymarks/WMN3PN_Brownie_the-railroad-dog-Vicotrville-California_USA/. Accessed May 14, 2022.

Weiser, Kathy. "Fort Benton—Birthplace of Montana." *Legends of America*. Last modified February 2017. https://www.legendsofamerica.com/mt-fortbenton/2/.

Werner, George C. "Colorado and Southern Railway." *Texas State Historical Association Handbook of Texas*. Last modified June 1, 1995. https://www.tshaonline.org/handbook/entries/-colorado-and-southern-railway.

"Where Hasn't Little Dog Gone." *Milwaukee Sentinel*, November 11, 1977.

Wilking, Clarence R. *The Railway Mail Service: U.S. Mail Railway Post Office*. Marietta, OH: Railway Mail Service Library, 1985. http://www.railwaymailservicelibrary.org/articles/THE_RMS.DOC.

Williams, Helena. "The LIRR's Best Friend." MTA, 2010. https://www.mta.info/news/2010/05/28/lirrs-best-friend.

Winch, Guy. "The Importance of Belonging to a Tribe: The Curative Powers of Group Identity." *Psychology Today*, February 19, 2020.

Wolmar, Christian. *The Great Railroad Revolution: The History of Trains in America*. New York: Public Affairs Books, 2012.

Woof Advisor. "Public Transport Pet Policies Across the USA." https://www.woofadvisor.com/blog/public-transit-pet-policies-usa/. Accessed May 15, 2022.

Worthington, Heather. *Miles of Smiles: The Story of Roxey, the Long Island Railroad Dog*. West Bayshore: Blue Marlin Publications, 2010.

Young, Michelle. "Meet the Adorable Dogs of the K9 Unit That Protect Amtrak at Penn Station." *Untapped New York*, August 28, 2018. https://untappedcities.com/2018/08/28/meet-the-adorable-dogs-of-the-k9-unit-that-protect-amtrak-at-penn-station/.

Young, Michelle. "Secret 'FDR Train Car' No Longer Beneath Grand Central (and Was Never His!)." *Untapped Cities*, December 12, 2019. https://untappedcities.com/2019/12/12/secret-fdr-train-car-no-longer-beneath-grand-central-and-was-never-his/.

Ziel, Ron, and George H. Foster. *Steel Rails to the Sunrise: The Long Island Railroad*. Nattituck, NY: American House, 1987.

Zimmerman, Karl. "The Who's Who of Grand Central's Secret Track 61: Franklin Delano Roosevelt, Alco PAs, Andy Warhol, and More." *Trains Magazine* (April 2012): 67–69.

Index

Numbers in **_bold italics_** indicate pages with illustrations.

Action Group for Better Architecture 39
Albany Columbus Day parade 24
American Veterinary Medical Association 121
AMTRAK and Illinois Department of Transportation Companion Pets Pilot Project 103
Annie (raildog) 53–**_59_**
Association of American Railroads 74
Atlantic Charter Conference 71
Auburn University Canine Detection Program 97

Barkers for Britain 71
Barlettani, Elvio 110, 113, 117
Barron, Joseph 87
Bay Area Rapid Transit (BART) 93, 97–98, 106
Beauchemin, Joseph (oral history) 16–17
Beck, Christian 107
Belgian Malinois 91, 95
belonging 1, 2, 5, 7, 20, 21, 100–101, 119, 122–124
Black Oak Station 87
bloodhounds 45–46, 49–51, 92
Bob (raildog) 86
Boomer Jack (raildog) 25–27
Borggren, Erica 104
boxcar boys and girls 64
Brownie (raildog) 83–87
Budd, Roy 36
Bummer (raildog) 86–87
Burdette, Loretta 57–58
Burlington Northern and Santa Fe (BNSF) 99–100

Campiglia Marittima 110–113
charity dogs 29–32

Charity London Jacks (raildogs) 29–32
Chicago and North Western Railroad 48
Cleveland, Grover 23
Coan, Michael 89–90
collecting dogs 29–32
Colorado Central Railroad 55
community dogs 7, 124
companion pets 103–109
Compassion (statue) 116
Conneaut (railcar) 74
connection (search for) 123
Corbin, Austin 37
crime on railroads 46–48

Daily Discovery (Colorado Museum of Discovery) 57
Davisson, Shirley 84
Demuth, Christopher 56
Dunham, Representative Jeff 103

Estern, Neil 77

Fala (raildog) 68–82; F.D.R. monument **_81_**; speech 73
family (search for) 123
Ferdinand Magellan 68–69, 73–75, **_80_**
fires (railroad cars) 15
Fort Benton 60, 62–67
Fort Collins 53–59
free roaming dog 6; _see also_ stray dogs

Garden City Station 34–35
Gaynor Special 50
German shepherds 89, 95, 97, 99, 100
ghost story (Fala) 77–79
Gold Coast Railroad Museum 77
golden retrievers 95
Goodwin, Doris Kearns 73
Grand Central Station 77

149

Index

The Grapes of Wrath 85
Great Falls Tribune 66
Great Northern Railroad 60–66
Great Snow Blockade 41
grief 69, 73, 76, 81, 119, 121–122

Hachi (raildog) *see* Hachiko
Hachiko (raildog) 117
Hassett, William 69, 75
Hawkins, Sir Henry 28
Hell Gate Bridge 38
Hess, Elsie 37
Hill, James Jerome 63
Hobo (raildog) 86
hoboes: dogs as 64, 122; humans as 64
homing abilities of dogs 125
Houston METRO 98
human animal bond 120–122
Hurricane Katrina 104
Hyde Park 69–73, 76–79

international railroads 110–118
Irish terrier 30

Jagger (raildog) 99
Jamestown 86
Johnson, W.L. 42
Jones, Sgt. Micah 95

Kashtanka 114
Kellogg, Mrs. Augustus 70
Kelly, John (station master) 23
Kerwick, John 52
King, Barbara J. 121
King of the Deadheads 22, 24
Kirkham, Robert E. 49, 51, 92
Klara, Robert 75

Labrador retrievers 29, 95
Lampo (raildog) 110–113, *117*
Ledford, Sgt. Jason 97
Levin, Sen. Carl 77
Lily (raildog) 103
London and Southwestern Railway Servants Orphanage 29–30
Long Island Railroad 33–52

Malchik 116
mascots (raildogs as) 5, 11, 13, 17, 18, 34, 42, 80, 83, 112
Maysville, Kentucky 9
McGrane, Sally 115
McSweeney, Pat 61
Merrick Station 34, 37, 42–43, 127

metaphor (dogs as) 19
Metro dogs 114
Metropolitan Transportation Authority (MTA) 38, 52, 88–90, 100, 108
Miles of Smiles (book) 43
Mineola Post Office 47
Mineola Village 47
Montana School for the Deaf and the Blind 65–66
monuments (to raildogs) 127–128
Moscow commuter dogs 113
Myers, Capt. Deborah 97

National Academies of Science, Engineering and Medicine study 93
National Police Canine Association 99
Nellie (raildog) 49
Neuronov, Andrei 115–116
New Yorker magazine 115
Norris, Phil 36
Northwestern Pacific Railroad 25–27

Owney (raildog) 9–21, **20**, 22–23, 25, 124, 127
Oyster Bay 33

Paddington Station 30
Pennsylvania Railroad Police Act 48–49
Pennsylvania Station 36, 39, **43**
Peters, Ralph 33, 34, 41
Pets on Trains Act 103
philanthropists (dogs as) 22, 29–32, 124
Pierce Arrow 78
Pinkerton, Allan 90
police dogs 91
polio (F.D.R.) 68
Port Authority of New York 93, 100
Port Authority Police Department Canine Unit 100
Portland Canine Corps 92
Poyarkov, Andrei 114
Prendergast, Thomas 89

Quebec conference (1944) 71

railroad detectives 45, 46, 49–51
Railroad Jack of Albany (raildog) 22–25; kidnapping 24
Railroad Jack of Lewes Station (raildog) 27–28
railroad police 48–49, 51, 90–91
Railroad Police Act of 1865 48
railway mail clerks 15–16
Reising, Frederick 46

Index

resilience (of raildogs) 57, 120, 122
romance of railroads 6, 120
Roosevelt, Eleanor 69, 73, 74, 76
Roosevelt, Franklin Delano 68–82
Route 66 Museum 83, 85
Roxey (raildog) 33–44, 127

St. Louis World's Fair 19
Sampson (raildog) 107
Schwarzman Animal Medical Center 88
Scottish terrier 68–69, 70–73, 79–80
search for home 5, 120–123
Sheba's Bob (raildog) 6, 45–52
sheepdog 60–62
sheepherders 60–62
Shep (raildog) 60–67; hero fund 65; monument 67
Shibuya train station 117
Shields, Ed 61–62, 65–66
Sierra Nevada Railroad 86
Slavik, Don 101
sleuth hound 49
Southeast Pennsylvania Transportation Authority (SEPTA) 98–99
Southern Railway Orphanage at Woking 29
Southwest Chief 84
station dogs 32
stray dogs 6–7, 20, 46, 113–118, 121, 123–124; *see also* free roaming dogs
street dogs (of Moscow) 113–117
Suckley, Margaret "Daisy" 70, 75–76
Summer (raildog) 95
Sunrise Trail Band 40

This Week (magazine) 113
Tim (raildog) 30, 97
Track 61 77–79
Trower, Officer Jackie 99
TSA 94
TSA National Explosive Detection Canine Program 94
Tully, Grace 72, 75–76
Tuolumne County 86
Turin Express 111
USS *Tuscaloosa* 71

United States Police Canine Association 94, 101
United States Railway Mail Service 9–20

vagabond dogs 2, 5–7, 10, 12, 14, 16, 37–38, 41, 64, 69, 110
Victorville 83
vigils 1, 7, 60, 64, 66, 117, 119

Wakefield, George 92
Waldorf Astoria 77
Wanamaker, John (postmaster) 13
Warm Springs 68–69, 71
Watrous, Ansel A. 55
Weimar, Dawn (sculptor) 58
Williams, Helena 44
Worthington, Heather Hill 43

YMCA (Long Island Branch) 34, 40

www.ingramcontent.com/pod-product-compliance
Ingram Content Group UK Ltd.
Pitfield, Milton Keynes, MK11 3LW, UK
UKHW042017140426
5217IPUK00015B/1215